GARY
RHODES
FOOD WITH FRIENDS

GARY
RHODES
FOOD WITH FRIENDS

EBURY PRESS
LONDON

First published in Great Britain in 2002

1 3 5 7 9 10 8 6 4 2

Copyright © Eaglemoss Publications Ltd 2002
Gary Rhodes original recipes © Gary Rhodes 2002
Front cover photograph © BBC 2002

First published by Ebury Press
Random House, 20 Vauxhall Bridge Road,
London SW1V 2SA

Random House Australia (Pty) Limited
20 Alfred Street, Milsons Point, Sydney, New South
Wales 2061, Australia

Random House New Zealand Limited
18 Poland Road, Glenfield, Auckland 10, New Zealand

Random House South Africa (Pty) Limited
Endulini, 5A Jubilee Road, Parktown 2193, South Africa

The Random House Group Limited Reg. No. 954009

www.randomhouse.co.uk

A CIP catalogue record for this book is available from
the British Library

ISBN 0 09 188668 6

This book was designed, edited and produced by
Eaglemoss Publications Ltd, based on the partwork
Good Cooking with Gary Rhodes

Printed and bound in Italy by De Agostini

contents

introduction

Sitting down to share great food, good wine and fun conversation with people you like is one of life's great pleasures. But spare a thought for the poor cook, working over a hot stove and missing out on all the fun.

That is why I've planned the menus in *Food with Friends* to make life as easy as possible for the person preparing the meal. All the recipes are designed to minimize fuss without sacrificing flavour. Even the shopping lists and preparation schedules are worked out for each menu leaving as little as possible to do at the last minute.

My selection of menus covers most eventualities, including hearty Sunday roasts, barbecues, sophisticated dinner parties and festive celebrations. I've organized them into three groups: menus for four diners, menus for six and – for when you feel like inviting a crowd – menus for six to eight and more. To keep everybody happy, there's something for fish lovers, vegetarians and meat-eaters in each chapter.

I hope this book will inspire a few dinner parties over the years.

essential information

kitchen safety

- Always wash your hands before preparing or handling food.

- Wash fresh produce before preparation.

- Prepare and store raw and cooked food separately.

- Clean work surfaces, chopping boards and utensils between preparing food which is to be cooked and food which is not.

- Put chilled and frozen foods into your fridge or freezer as soon as possible after purchase.

- Keep raw meat and fish at the bottom of your fridge.

- Keep the coldest part of your fridge at 0-5°C.

- If you are pregnant or elderly, avoid food that contains raw eggs.

- Check use by dates on packaging and keep to them.

- If reheating food, make sure that it's piping hot.

- Keep pets away from worktops and food dishes.

note on menus

Shopping lists cover the whole menu. If you want to cook just one dish, use the 'you will need' list with each recipe as a shopping guide. Quantities are not listed when a minimal amount is required.

notes on the recipes

- Measurements are given in both metric and imperial: do not mix the two.

- Spoon measurements are level.

- Tbsp and tsp are used for tablespoon and teaspoon: tbsp = 15ml, tsp = 5ml. An accurate set of measuring spoons helps to avoid mistakes.

- Season, unless otherwise stated, means seasoning with salt and freshly ground black pepper.

- Eggs are size 2 (large).

- Ingredients are listed with the most important first, then other ingredients in the order of use.

oven temperatures

Celsius	Fahrenheit	gas	description
110°C	250°F	1/4	Cool
120°C	250°F	1/2	Cool
140°C	275°F	1	Very low
150°C	300°F	2	Very low
160°C	325°F	3	Low
170°C	325°F	3	Moderate
180°C	350°F	4	Moderate
190°C	375°F	5	Moderately hot
200°C	400°F	6	Hot
220°C	425°F	7	Hot
230°C	450°F	8	Very hot

pastry

It is very satisfying to make your own pastry so, if you have the time, try out the recipes here. Otherwise, you can buy several types of ready-made or partly made pastry in most major supermarkets.

shortcrust pastry

makes 350g (12oz)
preparation time *10 minutes*
resting time *20 minutes after binding; 15 minutes after lining dish*
for **cooking times** and **oven temperatures** *follow individual recipes*

225g (8oz) plain flour
150g (5oz) chilled unsalted butter, chopped
1 egg, beaten (an extra egg yolk can be added for a stronger/richer flavour)

equipment
large mixing bowl
metal sieve
rolling pin, at least 30cm (12in) long
large marble slab or cool, smooth surface for rolling
pastry brush, for glazing the top of the pie with beaten egg
round pastry cutters, for making tartlets and individual cakes

making the dough
1 Sift the flour into a bowl. Rub the butter into the flour between your thumbs and fingertips until the mixture resembles coarse breadcrumbs (see picture **a**).
2 Add the beaten egg and mix it into the pastry crumbs with a round-bladed knife until they start to bind together. Then, using one hand, lightly gather the mixture together to form a soft, but not sticky ball of dough.
3 Wrap the ball of dough in plastic wrap and chill in the fridge for 20 minutes before starting to roll it out.

rolling the dough
1 Lightly flour the rolling pin and surface, both of which should be cool and dry. Starting from the centre, roll outwards, working in one direction only – usually away from you – using short strokes.
2 Regularly give the dough a quarter turn to prevent it from sticking and lift it occasionally to re-flour underneath.
3 Roll the dough out until it is about 3mm (⅛in) thick and forms a circle at least 5cm (2in) in diameter larger than the dish being lined.

lining the dish
1 Grease the dish before lining it. Wrap the pastry around the rolling pin, taking care not to stretch it, and unwind it over the dish. Try to line the dish evenly because this ensures that the pastry base holds the maximum amount of filling. Let the surplus pastry hang over the edge.

2 Supporting the edge of the pastry with one hand, press the sheet of dough gently down into the angle between the sides and the base with the other hand (see picture **b**).
3 Roll the rolling pin over the top of the dish to cut off the surplus dough or trim off the excess with a small knife.
4 With a fork, prick small holes across the pastry base to let any steam that forms underneath during baking escape.

variations
It's easy to make a variety of shortcrust pastries. Just add extra ingredients to the flour or use a different type of flour. For instance, for sweet shortcrust pastry, sift in 55g (2oz) of icing sugar; for pepper pastry, add 2 tbsp black pepper; and for wholemeal pastry, substitute 115g (4oz) of wholemeal flour for half the quantity of plain flour.

a

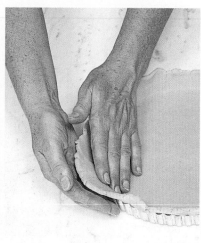
b

puff pastry

This recipe is simpler and quicker than the traditional method of making puff pastry. To minimize any chance of the butter softening or melting into the flour, chill all the ingredients and equipment before starting to make the dough.

makes about 675g (1½lb)

450g (1lb) plain flour, chilled

1 tsp salt

275g (10oz) butter, chilled until very hard and sliced into small pieces

300ml (10fl oz) iced water

making the dough

1 Sieve the flour with the salt into a mixing bowl.

2 Add the butter and water to the flour and salt in the bowl. Using two blunt knives, slice and fold the ingredients together without chopping up the butter too finely.

3 Gather the dough into a ball. Work quickly to avoid overhandling the dough and softening the butter. Cover with plastic wrap and refrigerate for 30 minutes.

rolling the dough

1 On a lightly floured surface, roll out the dough to a neat rectangle, 45cm (18in) long and 15cm (6in) wide. Roll the dough away from you, making sure it doesn't stick.

2 With the short side of the dough towards you, fold the top one-third into the middle. Then fold the bottom third over it to form a square of dough.

3 Turn the dough through 90° to bring the top seam to the left.

4 Gently press all the seams with the rolling pin to seal them. Leave to rest for 20 minutes in the fridge.

5 Repeat the rolling, folding and turning cycle three times. Let the dough rest for 20 minutes between each cycle.

stocks

Home-made versions of these store-cupboard essentials are best. If you have the time, make a fresh supply whenever you're running low and freeze it in small quantities. You can keep stocks in the freezer for two months. Alternatively, there are perfectly good ready-made versions in the chill cabinets of most major supermarkets. The third option is stock cubes – dissolve them in slightly more water than recommended (twice the amount for fish cubes) to combat the saltiness.

beef stock

An inexpensive cut of beef such as shin makes excellent stock. Browning the onions and vegetables first ensures a rich colour.

makes about 1.7 litres (3 pints)

1.8kg (4lb) shin of beef, cut into large pieces

2 large carrots, coarsely chopped

3 celery sticks, coarsely chopped

2 large onions, washed and unpeeled, cut into quarters

2 tbsp olive oil

1 leek, chopped

6 peppercorns

1 sprig of fresh thyme

1 bay leaf

1 Pre-heat the oven to 200°C/ 400°F/ gas 6. Roast the carrots and celery in the oven for 20 minutes, turning from time to time, until lightly browned.

2 While the vegetables are in the oven, heat the oil in a saucepan, minimum 4.5 litres (8 pints) capacity, and sweat the onions for 30 minutes, stirring occasionally, until richly browned.

3 Transfer the roasted vegetables to the saucepan. Lay the remaining ingredients on top and fill the pan to within 2.5cm (1in) of the rim with cold water.

4 Bring the stock to the boil slowly, skimming off any scum that floats to the top. Turn down the heat and simmer for 4 hours. Occasionally skim off any more scum that rises to the surface.

5 To strain the stock, ladle the liquid, vegetables and meat into a sieve or colander over a large bowl, jug or saucepan. For a really clear stock, line the sieve with a piece of clean muslin first.

fish stock

Turbot and sole bones make the best-flavoured stock, but plaice, cod, haddock, whiting, coley and salmon are excellent substitutes. Only use the freshest bones – don't use any which are soft or grey – and cut them into small pieces to extract more flavour from them. Remove the eyes and gills from fish heads because these will impair the stock's flavour and appearance. Avoid mackerel and herring because they produce an oily stock with a distinctive taste.

makes about 2 litres (3½ pints)

55g (2oz) unsalted butter
1 large onion, sliced
1 leek, sliced
2 celery sticks, sliced
a few stalks of fresh parsley
1 bay leaf
6 black peppercorns
900g (2lb) fish bones
300ml (10fl oz) dry white wine

1 Melt the butter in a large pan over a low heat. Tip in the onion, leek and celery and stir well.
2 Cook slowly for 3-4 minutes, or until the vegetables are softening but not coloured. Add the fresh parsley, bay leaf and black peppercorns.
3 Meanwhile, chop the fish bones with scissors and rinse under cold water. Add the bones to the pan and cook for a few more minutes.
4 Pour in the wine. Boil vigorously for 2-3 minutes until almost dry. Add 2.25 litres (4 pints) of water, bring to the boil and simmer for 20 minutes, removing any scum with a spoon.
5 Ladle the stock into a sieve set over a large bowl. Discard all the bones and vegetables. Leave to cool, then skim off any fat which settles on the surface.

chicken stock

You can use a raw chicken carcass, bony joints (wings or drumsticks are best) or a whole chicken to make this stock.

makes about 1.2 litres (2 pints)

0.9kg (2lb) raw chicken carcasses or joints
25g (1oz) unsalted butter
1 onion, peeled and chopped
1 celery stick, chopped
1 leek, cleaned and roughly chopped
3 black peppercorns
1 bay leaf
1 sprig of fresh thyme

1 In a large saucepan, melt the butter and lightly soften the onion, celery and leek, without letting them brown.
2 Add the chicken, peppercorns, bay leaf and thyme to the pot.
3 Cover with 1.5-2 litres (3-3½ pints) of water and bring slowly to the boil. With a metal spoon, skim off any scum that rises to the surface.
4 Reduce the heat and simmer for 2-3 hours, de-scumming occasionally.
5 Strain the stock through a sieve or colander set over a large bowl, jug or saucepan, and throw away the bones, herbs and vegetables.

gravy

Match the stock to the meat you are cooking (use chicken stock for turkey). Alternatively, use water left-over from boiled vegetables.

makes 600ml (1 pint)

residue from roast meat in the roasting tin
1-1½ tbsp plain flour
425-600ml (15fl oz-1 pint) hot stock or cooking water from boiled vegetables
75ml (2½fl oz) red or white wine (optional)
salt and pepper

1 Lift the joint out of the tin, along with any big pieces of onion or meat. Tilt the tin and skim off most of the fat with a metal spoon. Scrape the tin to loosen any residue.
2 Place the tin over a low heat. When the fat sizzles, add the flour and stir very quickly with a flat whisk or wooden spoon until the flour is blended and the mixture is smooth.
3 Gradually add the stock or cooking water, stirring constantly. Stir in the wine, if using. Simmer and stir until the gravy thickens to the desired consistency. Season with salt and pepper to taste.

chapter one
menus for four

tastes of the sea

serves 4

mussel chowder

crispy salmon
with tomato and sweet pepper sauce

lemon jelly
with frosted grapes

This is a menu for a special occasion. The mussel chowder has a deep satisfying flavour while the crisp, moist salmon is served with a zingy tomato and sweet pepper sauce. Clean-tasting lemon jelly makes a refreshing end to the meal.

Shopping list

1 carrot
1 leek
2 large potatoes
5 large onions
4 large shallots (or 1 onion)
3 celery sticks
4 tomatoes
900g (2lb) spinach
450g (1lb) baby or new potatoes
7 lemons
small bunch of green seedless grapes
fresh parsley
fresh tarragon
450g (1lb) fresh mussels
4-6 rashers streaky bacon
4 x 175g (6oz) salmon fillet portions, scaled
225g (8oz) unsalted butter
300ml (10fl oz) milk
150ml (5fl oz) single cream
1 egg
300ml (10fl oz) passata
210g (7½oz) can sweet red peppers
capers (in brine)
1 bay leaf
green peppercorns (in brine)
1 glass white wine
750ml (1¼ pints) fish stock (see page 10)
315g (11oz) caster sugar
2 x 11.7g sachets powdered gelatine or
3 x 6g vegetarian gelatine
olive oil

Prepare ahead

The day before

Make the jelly and refrigerate

Make the tomato and sweet pepper sauce (without the herbs) and refrigerate

On the day

2 hours before guests arrive

Chop all the vegetables for the soup

Wash and trim the stems from the spinach

Dip the frosted grapes and put them in the fridge

1 hour before guests arrive

Make the soup and keep it warm

Score the salmon skin

30 minutes before guests arrive

Prepare the potatoes and put them in the oven

Between the starter and main course

Sear the salmon steaks

Reheat the tomato and sweet pepper sauce and add the chopped herbs

Cook the spinach

Between the main course and pudding

Un-mould the jellies

Safety first

- When buying mussels, avoid any that feel heavy (these are full of sand) or seem loose when shaken (these are probably dead).
- Mussels must be alive until used. To check, tap gently with a knife – the shells should instantly be pulled tightly shut.
- Keep shellfish in the fridge and use on the day of purchase.
- Do not eat shellfish that you collect at the seaside – many shorelines are polluted.
- Do not eat any mussels that are still closed after cooking.

3 Discard any mussels which are open, cracked or do not shut when tapped (see 'Safety first' on page 14).
4 Soak the mussels in a bowl of lightly salted cold water for 2 hours to remove any impurities.

cooking the mussels
1 Melt the butter in a pan, add the vegetables and bay leaf and fry gently until they just begin to soften. Add the white wine and boil until almost dry; add the stock and bring back to the boil.
2 Add the mussels to the boiling stock, cover and cook for 5-8 minutes until the shells open. Discard any that do not open.
3 Lift out the mussels with a slotted spoon and reserve the stock for the chowder.

making the chowder
1 Melt the butter in a large pan. Add the streaky bacon and fry until golden.
2 Add the diced potatoes, onions and celery and cook gently for 4-5 minutes.
3 Add the reserved stock and simmer for about 15 minutes until the potato is cooked but not falling apart.
4 Add the hot milk and single cream and simmer, then season with salt and pepper to taste.
5 Shell all but 12 of the mussels and drop them into the soup. Warm through for 1-2 minutes. Serve with 3 reserved mussels in their shells in each bowl.

mussel chowder

This soup is deliciously rich with a wonderful taste of the sea. It makes an excellent starter for a dinner party – or a great supper for two – served with fresh white bread and unsalted butter.

you will need
preparation time
20 minutes

cooking time
40 minutes

for the mussels
450g (1lb) fresh mussels, washed and bearded
25g (1oz) unsalted butter
1 carrot, roughly chopped
1 onion, roughly chopped
1 celery stick, chopped
½ leek, roughly chopped
1 bay leaf

1 glass white wine
750ml (1¼ pints) fish stock (see page 10) or water

for the chowder
55g (2oz) butter
4-6 rashers streaky bacon, cut into 2.5cm (1in) strips
2 large potatoes, cut into 2cm (¾in) dice
3-4 large onions, cut into 2cm (¾in) dice
2 celery sticks, cut into 2cm (¾in) dice
300ml (10fl oz) hot milk

150ml (5fl oz) single cream
salt and pepper

cleaning the mussels
1 Use the unsharpened edge of a knife to scrape off any barnacles attached to the shells, and to pull off the beard-like fibres. (As a safety precaution, move the knife away from you as you work.)
2 Scrub the mussels well under running water.

crispy salmon
with tomato and sweet pepper sauce

Pan-fried salmon looks impressive, tastes utterly delicious and is very easy to make. The fish has an ultra-crispy skin but tender flesh and sits on a bed of tasty tomato and sweet pepper sauce. Serve with buttered spinach and potatoes.

Cook's notes

To give each piece of salmon a very crispy skin, lightly score the skin, then lay the fillet, skin-side down in a hot pan and leave it to cook for at least 5 minutes. Resist the temptation to move the fish around or to take a peep to see how it is progressing. Cooked in this manner, the crispy skin becomes the tastiest treat on the plate!

you will need

preparation time *25 minutes*
cooking time *15 minutes for the sauce; 8 minutes for the salmon fillets*

for the fish
4 x 175g (6oz) salmon fillets, scaled
1 tbsp olive oil
knob of butter
salt and pepper
sprigs of tarragon, to serve

for the sauce
4 tomatoes, peeled and deseeded
210g (7½oz) can sweet red peppers
1 tbsp olive oil
4 large shallots or 1 onion, chopped
300ml (10fl oz) passata
1 tsp green peppercorns (in brine)
1 lemon, peeled and sliced
3 tsp capers, chopped
salt and pepper
1 tsp chopped fresh parsley
1 heaped tsp chopped fresh tarragon

for the potatoes
450g (1lb) baby or new potatoes
4-6 tbsp olive oil

25g (1oz) butter
salt and pepper

for the spinach
900g (2lb) spinach, washed and trimmed
55g (2oz) butter
juice of half a lemon

making the sauce
1 Warm the olive oil in a medium pan and add the chopped shallots or onion. Cook on a medium heat for 1-2 minutes until softened.
2 Add the passata and green peppercorns, bring to a simmer and cook for 2-3 minutes.
3 Cut the tomato and sweet peppers into 1cm (½in) dice.
4 Add the lemon, capers, tomatoes and sweet peppers. Simmer for 1 minute and season. Add the parsley and tarragon just before serving.

pan-frying the salmon
1 Lightly score the skin of the salmon and season.

2 Heat the olive oil in a frying-pan over a moderate heat. Place the salmon skin side down in the oil and leave for 5 minutes. (Check occasionally that it is not burning.)
3 Add the butter to the pan, turn the salmon over and finish cooking for 2-3 minutes (less for a thin fillet).

cooking the vegetables
1 Pre-heat the oven to 200°C/400°F/gas 6. Parboil the potatoes for 4 minutes, then drain. Tip into a roasting tin, drizzle with olive oil, dot with butter and season. Roast in the oven for 30-40 minutes.
2 Cook the damp spinach in butter in a large pan over a medium heat for 4-5 minutes, stirring occasionally, until it wilts. Add the lemon juice and season just before serving.

to serve
Spoon the sauce on to warmed plates and put the salmon, skin side up, in the centre of each plate. Garnish with sprigs of tarragon.

lemon jelly
with frosted grapes

H ome-made jelly, full of natural flavour, is a treat to be savoured. These sweet individual lemon jellies are adorned with pretty frosted grapes.

you will need

preparation time *30 minutes*

setting time *6-8 hours or overnight*

for the jelly

5 lemons, scrubbed, zested and juiced

275g (10oz) caster sugar

2 x 11.7g sachets powdered gelatine

for the frosted grapes

small bunch of green seedless grapes

1 egg white

25g (1oz) caster sugar

making the jelly

1 Check that you have at least 4 small decorative moulds – large enough to hold 150ml (5fl oz) – in which to set the jelly.

2 Warm the sugar, 600ml (1 pint) water, lemon juice and zest gently in a pan until the sugar dissolves. Keep heating for a further 2-3 minutes.

3 Take off the heat and sprinkle over the powdered gelatine. Leave for 2-3 minutes until it becomes spongy.

4 Return the pan to a very low heat and warm for 2-3 minutes until the gelatine melts. Do not let it boil.

5 Strain the mixture through a nylon sieve and then through muslin (for a very clear jelly).

6 Let the jelly cool, stirring occasionally, then pour into the moulds. Leave to set in the fridge.

frosting the grapes

Put the sugar on a plate, and the egg white in a small bowl. Dunk the grapes – individually or in small bunches – into the egg, then dredge them in the sugar and set aside to dry.

to serve

To un-mould the jellies, dip the base of the moulds into warm water for 10 seconds and turn out. Decorate each plate with a few frosted grapes.

stylish
supper
serves 4

angels on horseback
chased by devils on horseback

pan-fried skate wings
with peppers, potatoes and Bayonne ham

roast peaches
with blueberry ripple ice-cream

The fishy starter and main course in this elegant dinner work well together. The oysters contrast with the sweet, moist prunes and the bacon adds a salty dimension. Skate wings make a light, yet substantial, main course, garnished with peppers, capers and Bayonne ham to provide a hint of the Mediterranean. Roasting peaches intensifies their flavour, and blueberry ripple ice-cream is a perfect accompaniment for this stunning dessert.

Shopping list

2 red peppers
225-350g (8-12oz) new potatoes
mixed salad leaves
lamb's lettuce
few sprigs of flatleaf parsley
4 large or 8 small ripe peaches
250g (9oz) ripe blueberries plus extra for garnish
8 no-soak stoned dried prunes
2 lemons
8 rashers of rindless streaky bacon
4-6 slices Bayonne ham
8 oysters
4 x 225-280g (8-10oz) skate wings
1 tbsp plain flour
115g (4oz) unsalted butter
600ml (1 pint) vanilla ice-cream
4 slices bread
bread rolls
5-6 tbsp olive oil
25g (1oz) soft, light brown sugar
55g (2oz) icing sugar
2 tbsp vinaigrette dressing (see page 22)
4 tbsp mango chutney
12 caper berries

Prepare ahead

The day before
Make the blueberry coulis and chill it
Fold the coulis into the ice-cream and return the ice-cream to the freezer

On the day

2-3 hours before guests arrive
Prepare the angels and devils on horseback, cover and store in the fridge

1 hour before guests arrive
Roast the peaches, transfer from the roasting tin and cover
Boil the potatoes, slice and toss in the lemon dressing; fry the peppers

Just before sitting down to eat
Cook the angels and devils in the pre-heated oven
Toast the bread discs

Between the starter and main course
Cook the skate and assemble the salad

Between the main course and pudding
Glaze the peaches

down, in a cloth. Insert the tip of a knife at the pointed end and slide it along the bottom shell. Twist the shell to open.

2 Detach the strong muscle which opens and closes the shell and scrape out the oyster.

making the angels and devils

1 Pre-heat the oven to 200°C/400°F/gas 6.

2 On a chopping board, stretch each rasher of bacon with the back of a knife (this helps to prevent shrinking during cooking).

3 Cut each rasher in half lengthways; wrap half a rasher around each oyster or prune.

4 Place the oyster and prune rolls on separate baking sheets, tightly packed side by side to prevent them unravelling, and bake for 8 minutes.

assembling the dish

1 Pre-heat the grill. Cut the bread into eight 5-6cm (2-2½in) discs using a small ring mould or biscuit cutter. Toast them under the grill.

2 Butter the toast discs and arrange two on each serving plate. Place 2 angels on one disc and 2 devils on the other. Garnish with lamb's lettuce and 1 tbsp mango chutney on each plate.

angels on horseback
chased by devils on horseback

The oysters and prunes are wrapped in bacon, baked in the oven and served on crispy toasted discs of bread accompanied by mango chutney. The quantities given here make 8 angels and 8 devils.

you will need

preparation time
10 minutes

cooking time *8 minutes*

4 slices of bread
butter for spreading
lamb's lettuce for garnish
4 tbsp mango chutney

for the angels
8 oysters, opened and removed from shells
4 rashers of rindless streaky bacon

for the devils
8 no-soak stoned prunes

4 rashers of rindless streaky bacon

opening the oysters
1 Clean the oysters in the same way as the mussels (see 'cleaning the mussels' on page 15). Hold an oyster, rounded side

pan-fried skate wings
with peppers, potatoes and Bayonne ham

Skate wings are perfect for this dish as they are moist and flavourful. The wings are pan-fried briefly and served on a bed of warm new potatoes, softened red pepper and mixed salad leaves topped with crispy, smoky Bayonne ham. If you can't buy Bayonne ham, use Parma ham instead.

you will need

preparation time *5 minutes*

cooking time *10 minutes*

for the skate

4 x 225-280g (8-10oz) skate wings

1 tbsp plain flour

25g (1oz) unsalted butter, melted

salt and pepper

4-6 thin slices Bayonne ham, cut into 1cm (1/2in) wide strips

for the potato and pepper salad

225-350g (8-12oz) new potatoes

2 red peppers, deseeded and cut into 1cm (1/2in) wide slices

juice of 1 lemon

5-6 tbsp olive oil

salt and pepper

12 caper berries

to serve

mixed salad leaves

2 tbsp vinaigrette dressing (see right)

sprigs of flatleaf parsley

crusty rolls and butter

preparing the salad

1 Boil the new potatoes until tender, then drain and cool. Cut into 1cm (1/2in) thick slices.

2 Whisk the lemon juice with 4 tbsp olive oil and season. Pour the mix over the potatoes.

3 Fry the pepper slices in a little of the remaining olive oil until slightly

vinaigrette dressing
makes 600ml (1 pint)

300ml (10fl oz) extra virgin olive oil

300ml (10fl oz) groundnut oil

25ml (1fl oz) balsamic vinegar

1 bunch fresh basil

1/2 bunch fresh tarragon

3-4 sprigs fresh thyme

12 black peppercorns, lightly crushed

3 shallots, finely chopped

2 garlic cloves, crushed

1 bay leaf

1 tsp coarse sea salt

coloured and just softening.

4 Add the pepper to the potato slices, mix well and then add the caper berries.

pan-frying the skate wings

1 Dust the skate wings with the flour, brush with the melted butter and season with salt and pepper.

2 Heat the frying-pan, pour in a little olive oil and fry the ham until crisp. Keep warm on a plate.

3 Add the skate wings to the pan, pale side down. Fry for 2 minutes, turn and cook for a further minute.

to serve

Put one skate wing, pale side up, on each plate, with a little of the potato and pepper salad. Toss the salad leaves in the vinaigrette and arrange beside the skate. Top each wing with crisp, crumpled ham and a sprig of parsley. Serve with crusty rolls and butter.

1 Warm the olive and groundnut oils together in a pan. Push all the remaining ingredients into a 750ml (1 1/4 pint) bottle.

2 Pour the warm oils into the bottle, seal with a cork or screw top, then shake to mix.

3 For the tastiest results, leave the oil, herbs and garlic to marinate for up to a week. To help the flavours develop, shake the bottle once a day. At the end of the week, check the seasoning, strain the vinaigrette into a clean bottle and store in the fridge.

roast peaches
with blueberry ripple ice-cream

This is a modern twist on the popular peach melba. For a simpler dessert, you could serve the roast peaches with vanilla ice-cream sitting in a pool of blueberry coulis.

you will need

preparation time 15 minutes

cooking time 20-25 minutes

4 large or 8 small peaches, skins on

250g (9oz) ripe blueberries

2 tbsp lemon juice

55g (2oz) icing sugar

600ml (1 pint) vanilla ice-cream

55g (2oz) butter

25g (1oz) soft, light brown sugar

a few fresh blueberries for garnish

making the coulis

1 Put the blueberries in a bowl with the lemon juice and blitz with a hand-blender until smooth.

2 Push the purée through a metal sieve with a wooden spoon.

3 Sieve the icing sugar into the mixture and stir thoroughly. If necessary, add more sugar to taste.

rippling the ice-cream

1 Put the vanilla ice-cream in the fridge to soften slightly.

2 When the ice-cream is soft enough to stir easily, start slicing cleanly through it with a metal spoon. Drizzle the blueberry coulis into the furrow behind the spoon. Repeat several times, until all the coulis is marbled into the ice-cream. (Fold rather than stir the coulis into the ice-cream to get clear stripes, not purple ice.) Refreeze the ice-cream.

roasting the peaches

1 Pre-heat the oven to 200°C/400°F/gas 6.

2 Heat an ovenproof frying-pan with 25g (1oz) of the butter. Add the peaches and cook for 4-5 minutes until they start to become golden brown, turning occasionally.

3 Transfer the peaches to the oven and roast for 15-20 minutes. Then remove and discard the skins and transfer the peaches to a plate.

4 Pour off any excess butter from the pan and wipe clean. Add the remaining butter with the sugar and 4tbsp water. Bring to a simmer and add the peaches to the pan. Reduce the syrup while rolling the peaches in it to coat them with a shiny glaze.

5 Serve one or two warm peaches per portion with a scoop of ice-cream and a few fresh blueberries. Trickle any syrup over the peaches.

flavours of Provence

serves 4

cod brandade
with toasted French bread

chicken Provençal
with slow-baked pommes Anna

crispy apple tarts

Provençal cooking is predominantly flavoured with olive oil, olives, garlic and tomatoes, and this menu makes good use of these ingredients. Cod brandade, a subtle, garlicky dip, is an ideal starter to contrast with the richness of chicken Provençal. Delectably sweet apples on a wafer-thin pastry base provide a classic dessert.

Shopping list

675g (1½lb) waxy potatoes
1 large onion
2 lemons
8 Granny Smith apples
5 garlic cloves
fresh basil
fresh thyme
4 boneless chicken breast fillets
450g (1lb) salt cod
140g (5oz) butter
150ml (5fl oz) whipping cream or apple sorbet (see page 31)
225g (8oz) puff pastry (see page 9)
1 stick of French bread
2 thick slices white bread
2 tbsp plain flour
5 tbsp black olives
2 x 400g cans chopped tomatoes
4-5 tbsp mayonnaise (see page 187)
6 black peppercorns
8 tbsp olive oil
500ml (18fl oz) red wine
4 tsp caster sugar
4 tbsp apricot jam

Prepare ahead

The day before

Soak the salt cod overnight in cold water

On the day

In the morning

Cook the chicken Provençal but do not add the olives and basil leaves; cool, cover and store in the fridge. Make the cod brandade, cover and store in the fridge

2 hours before guests arrive

Assemble the pommes Anna and place in the oven to cook
Roll out the pastry discs for the apple tarts and store in the fridge
Slice the apples, sprinkle with lemon juice to stop discolouring and keep in the fridge

30 minutes before eating

Take the pommes Anna out of the oven. Turn the oven up to 220°C/425°F/gas 7
Assemble and bake the apple tarts

Just before sitting down to eat

Remove the apple tarts from the oven. Turn off the oven but put in the pommes Anna to warm through; gently reheat the chicken
Garnish the brandade with black olives and toast bread slices to serve with it

Between the starter and main course

Add the olives and basil leaves to the chicken

Between the main course and pudding

Whip the cream to serve with the warm apple tarts

(see page 187)

Cook's notes

When you buy salt cod at a fishmonger, delicatessen or supermarket, don't be put off by its stiff, dry and grey appearance – you'll be amazed at how 24 hours soaking softens and transforms the fish. For the best fish, ask for chunky pieces from the middle of the fillet rather than thin tail or gill ends.

and bring to the boil. Simmer for 4 minutes. Remove from the heat and leave it to go on cooking in its own juice as it cools.
3 Drain the cod and remove the skin and bones.
4 Soak the bread in a little water with 1 tbsp of the olive oil. Squeeze out the excess water.
5 Put the salt cod, bread and garlic into a food processor. Gradually add the remaining oil and whizz until it is thoroughly incorporated.
6 Add the rest of the lemon juice and salt and pepper to taste. Stir in the mayonnaise and season with more salt and pepper if required.
7 Pile into individual serving dishes and garnish with the olives.

to serve
Brush the bread slices with olive oil on both sides and toast under the grill until golden. Use to dip into the brandade.

cod brandade

This is a delicious dip, with a creamy texture and light flavour. Here it is garnished with olives and served in the traditional way with toasted bread brushed with olive oil.

you will need
preparation time
5-10 minutes plus soaking time for the cod
cooking time
4 minutes plus cooling

for the brandade
450g (1lb) salt cod
juice of 2 lemons
6 black peppercorns
4-5 tbsp olive oil

2 thick slices white bread, crusts removed
2 garlic cloves, crushed
salt and pepper
4-5 tbsp mayonnaise (see page 187)

to garnish
1 tbsp pitted black olives
8 thin slices French bread
olive oil

making the brandade
1 Soak the salt cod in cold water for 24 hours. Change the water at least twice to ensure that as much salt as possible is extracted.
2 Drain the fish on absorbent kitchen paper. Place in a pan of cool water; add half the lemon juice and the peppercorns

chicken Provençal
with slow-baked pommes Anna

Tender pieces of chicken are cooked in a tomato and wine sauce and then garnished liberally with olives and torn basil leaves. Slow-baked pommes Anna, thinly sliced potato cooked with butter and thyme, give a genuine taste of Provence to accompany the chicken.

Cook's notes

For a change, replace the chicken with 4 thick pieces of cod. Soften the garlic and onion in the olive oil, add the tomatoes and wine and simmer for 10 minutes. Place the fish in a shallow baking dish, season and pour over the sauce. Cover with foil and bake in the oven at 190°C/375°F/gas 5 for 25 minutes or until cooked. Serve garnished with the olives and torn basil leaves.

you will need

preparation time
10 minutes for the chicken;
10 minutes for the potatoes

cooking time
10 minutes for the chicken;
1½ hours for the potatoes

for the chicken
4 boneless chicken breast fillets
2 tbsp plain flour
salt and pepper
1 tbsp butter
3 tbsp olive oil
1 large onion, chopped
2-3 garlic cloves, crushed
2 x 400g cans chopped tomatoes
500ml (18fl oz) red wine
4 tbsp pitted black olives
fresh basil leaves, torn

for the pommes Anna
675g (1½lb) waxy potatoes, peeled
55g (2oz) butter, melted
4 tbsp fresh thyme, chopped
salt and pepper

cooking the chicken
1 Season the flour and sift into a bowl. Remove the skin from the chicken and cut each into 2.5cm (1in) cubes. Roll in the flour to coat.
2 Melt the butter and heat the oil together in a pan. Add the chicken pieces, onion and garlic and cook for 3-4 minutes or until the chicken is lightly browned on each side.
3 Add the tomatoes and wine, mix well and cover. Reduce the heat and continue to cook for 8-10 minutes or until the meat is no longer pink and the juices run clear. Stir in the olives and torn basil leaves and serve.

cooking the pommes Anna
1 Pre-heat the oven to 190°C/375°F/gas 5. Brush a shallow 1 litre (1¾ pint) ovenproof dish with a little of the melted butter.
2 Slice the peeled potatoes as thinly as possible and pat them dry with kitchen paper.

3 Arrange a layer of potatoes over the base in concentric circles, neatly overlapping each slice. Brush with a little butter and sprinkle over a little thyme. Season if necessary.
4 Continue layering, brushing with butter and adding thyme and seasoning, until all the potatoes have been used.
5 Brush the top layer of potato slices with butter, cover with baking foil and cook in the oven for 1½ hours or until tender. Press down the potato slices 3-4 times during baking to form a firm cake. Slice into portions and serve.

Tip To intensify the flavour, you can cook the chicken the day before, without garnishing it. Gently reheat, either on a low heat on the hob or in a moderate oven, and garnish before serving.

crispy apple tarts

These tarts are so thin and crisp, you can fold them up and eat them in three or four bites. They eat well with lightly whipped cream, but are even tastier served with a spoonful of apple sorbet.

you will need

preparation time 15 minutes
cooking time 15-20 minutes

225g (8oz) puff pastry (see page 9)
55g (2oz) butter
8 Granny Smith apples, peeled, cored and quartered
4 tsp caster sugar
4 tbsp apricot jam
150ml (5fl oz) whipping cream, whipped or apple sorbet (see 'Recipe option' above)

1 Pre-heat the oven to 220°C/425°F/gas 7 and butter 2 large baking trays.
2 Roll out the pastry as thinly as possible and leave it to rest in a cool place. Cut it into four 20cm (8in) discs. Lay the pastry discs on the baking trays and leave them to rest in the fridge.
3 Cut each apple quarter into 4-5 slices, and arrange on top of the pastry discs. Start by placing them around the outside edge, overlapping the slices. Do the same in the middle of the pastry. To finish, sit 2-3 slices of apple in the centre.
4 Chop the butter and dot it over the tarts. Sprinkle each with caster sugar and bake for 15-20 minutes or until the pastry is crisp and the apples have started to colour.
5 Boil the apricot jam with 2tbsp water until they are combined. Brush liberally over each tart to give a rich glazed finish. Serve with whipped cream or apple sorbet (see above).

Recipe option

apple sorbet

6 Granny Smith apples, peeled, cored and quartered
300ml (10fl oz) sweet cider
55g (2oz) caster sugar

1 Mix all the ingredients together in a saucepan and simmer until the apples are tender. Drain off any excess liquid and purée the softened apple in a blender. Check for sweetness: if it is too tart, return to a simmer and add a little more sugar to taste. Leave to cool.
2 Churn in an ice-cream machine until thick and almost frozen. Leave to set in the freezer.
3 Remove the sorbet from the freezer and allow to soften for 30 minutes at room temperature before serving.

Spanish fiesta

serves 4

three tasty tapas
garlic mushrooms, prawns and salmorejo

chicken and pork paella
with a crisp green salad

Seville orange sponge

O ne good way to start a Spanish-inspired meal is to serve a selection of tempting tapas – garlicky mushrooms, sizzling prawns and salmorejo, a gazpacho-like tomato and bread dip. A rich and colourful paella with pieces of tender chicken and pork is followed by a sponge pudding flavoured with Seville oranges.

Shopping list

115g (4oz) mixed green salad leaves
½ cucumber
3 celery sticks
250g (8oz) oyster or button mushrooms
175g (6oz) green beans
450g (1lb) tomatoes
2 tomatoes
55g (2oz) mild green chillies
1 red chilli
6 garlic cloves
3 oranges
1 lemon
fresh rosemary
1 small bunch fresh parsley
1-2 slices Serrano ham
450g (1lb) chicken breast fillets
450g (1lb) lean pork
12 large raw prawns
55g (2oz) butter
4 tbsp milk
3 eggs
1 loaf white bread
750g (1lb 10oz) short or medium grain rice
85g (3oz) can butter beans
85g (3oz) self-raising flour
115g (4oz) caster sugar
5 tbsp Seville orange marmalade
olive oil
extra virgin olive oil
sherry vinegar
vinaigrette dressing (see page 22)
saffron
paprika

Prepare ahead

The day before

Cook the garlic mushrooms

Make the salmorejo and drizzle with olive oil but do not garnish; cover and store in the fridge

Make the orange custard, cover with greaseproof paper and put in the fridge

Dice the meat and cut the vegetables for the paella, cover and refrigerate

Make the salad and place in the fridge but do not add the dressing

On the day

30 minutes before guests arrive

Mix up the orange pudding

Just before sitting down to eat

Place the orange pudding in the oven to cook

Remove the garlic mushrooms from the fridge and garnish the salmorejo with the chopped ham

Cook the sizzling prawns

Start cooking the paella

Between the starter and main course

Finish cooking the paella, garnish with rosemary and leave to rest

Remove the salad from the fridge and add the dressing

Between the main course and pudding

Glaze the orange pudding

Gently warm the custard

garlic mushrooms
you will need
preparation time *5 minutes*

cooking time *3 minutes*

250g (8oz) button or oyster mushrooms

3 tbsp olive oil

3 garlic cloves, finely chopped

juice of ½ lemon

salt and pepper

2 tbsp parsley, chopped

1 Trim and wipe the mushrooms.

2 Heat the oil in a pan, add the mushrooms and garlic and fry over a high heat for 2-3 minutes.

3 Add the lemon juice, season and stir. Sprinkle with parsley. Serve hot or cold.

sizzling prawns
you will need
preparation time *5 minutes*

cooking time *5 minutes*

3 tbsp olive oil

1 garlic clove, chopped

1 red chilli, deseeded and chopped

pinch of paprika

12 raw prawns, shelled but with tails on

1 Heat the oil, garlic, chilli and paprika in a small pan.

2 Add the prawns and cook for 2-3 minutes or until pink and slightly curled.

three tasty tapas

Garlic mushrooms, sizzling prawns and salmorejo are delicious served with crusty bread and a glass of chilled dry sherry.

salmorejo
you will need
preparation time

15 minutes

225g (8oz) day-old bread

450g (1lb) ripe tomatoes, skinned, deseeded and chopped

55g (2oz) mild green chillies

2 garlic cloves, crushed

1 egg, beaten

salt and pepper

125ml (4fl oz) extra virgin olive oil plus extra, to serve

2½-3 tbsp sherry vinegar

1-2 slices Serrano ham, cut into thin strips

1 Cut off crusts and tear the bread into chunks. Cover with water and soak for 2 minutes; squeeze out the excess water. Place the bread in a food processor.

2 Deseed the chillies and chop the flesh.

3 Add the tomatoes, chillies and garlic to the bread and process until smooth. Add the beaten eggs, season and process until thick.

4 With the motor running, add the oil in a thin stream. Pour in the sherry vinegar and blend.

5 Serve the paste in a shallow bowl scattered with ham and drizzled with a little more olive oil.

chicken and pork paella
with a crisp green salad

Chicken and pork are the main ingredients in this version of the traditional Spanish rice dish, which is packed full of flavour. With the addition of green beans, tomatoes and butter beans, it's almost a meal in itself. A crisp, clean-tasting green salad is the ideal accompaniment.

Cook's notes

The three basic ingredients of paella are rice, saffron and olive oil but you can vary the other ingredients to suit individual tastes.

For a seafood inspired paella, omit the pork from the recipe below and substitute 175g (6oz) squid cut into thin strips and 140g (5oz) cooked, shelled prawns. Add these to the pan once the chicken is browned, and complete the recipe steps.

you will need

| preparation time | 15 minutes |
| cooking time | 30 minutes |

for the paella

450g (1lb) chicken breast fillets
450g (1lb) lean pork
175g (6oz) green beans, topped and tailed, strings removed
115g (4oz) canned butter beans
4-5 tbsp olive oil
2 ripe tomatoes, peeled and chopped
2 tsp paprika
½ tsp saffron
salt and pepper
750g (1lb 10oz) short or medium grain rice
2 sprigs fresh rosemary

for the green salad

115g (4oz) mixed green salad leaves
½ cucumber
3 celery sticks
vinaigrette dressing (see page 22)

cooking the paella

1 Remove any skin from the chicken fillets. Cut the chicken and pork into 2.5cm (1in) chunks.
2 Slice the prepared green beans into 2.5cm (1in) lengths. Drain the butter beans and rinse under cold running water.
3 Heat the oil in a large frying-pan, add the diced meat and cook until lightly browned.
4 Add the tomatoes, butter beans and sliced green beans. Stir to combine. Sprinkle with the paprika and saffron and season.
5 Add the rice, stir well and add 1.4-1.7 litres (2½-3 pints) water. Cook on a high heat for 10 minutes; reduce the heat and cook for another 10 minutes or until the rice is tender.
6 Roughly chop the rosemary sprigs and sprinkle over the top of the paella. Cover with a lid and leave the paella to rest for 5 minutes before serving.

making the green salad

1 Rinse and drain the salad leaves, then tear them into a serving bowl.
2 Halve the cucumber lengthways and remove the ends. Slice thinly.
3 Trim the ends of the celery sticks and cut into even lengths. Add to the salad leaves with the cucumber.
4 Just before serving, add the vinaigrette dressing and toss to coat.

Tip

If the paella dries out during cooking, add a little more water. If, however, the paella is still wet when the rice is cooked, increase the heat to evaporate excess liquid, taking care not to burn it.

You can also cook the paella in the oven. Pre-heat the oven to 160°C/325°F/gas 3. Prepare the paella to the end of step 3. Put the pan into the oven and cook, covered, for 20-25 minutes or until the rice is tender and the meat is cooked through.

Seville orange sponge

This glorious sponge pudding is flavoured with orange and has a Seville marmalade glaze. It eats very well with an orange custard.

you will need

preparation time *10-15 minutes*

cooking time *40-45 minutes*

juice of 2 oranges
55g (2oz) butter
115g (4oz) caster sugar
grated zest of 1 orange
2 eggs, separated
85g (3oz) self-raising flour
5 tbsp Seville orange marmalade
4 tbsp milk

1 Pre-heat the oven to 190°C/375°F/gas 5. Butter a 900ml (1½ pint) pudding dish.
2 Boil the orange juice to reduce by two-thirds, then leave to cool.
3 Cream together the butter and caster sugar with the orange zest. Stir in the egg yolks, then the self-raising flour.
4 Add 3 tbsp marmalade, milk and the reduced orange juice. Stir to combine.
5 Whisk the egg whites until they form soft peaks and gently fold into the pudding mix.

6 Spoon into the dish and place the dish in a roasting tin. Pour hot water into the tin, approximately 1cm (½in) deep.
7 Bake in the pre-heated oven for 40-45 minutes until golden brown.

finishing the sponge

To give an attractive glaze, mix 2 tbsp marmalade with 3-4 tsp water and warm through. Brush the glaze over the sponge and serve with orange custard, if liked (see 'Recipe option' above).

Recipe option

orange custard
makes 350ml (12fl oz)

4 egg yolks
40g (1½oz) caster sugar
150ml (5fl oz) milk
150ml (5fl oz) double cream
1 vanilla pod
zest of 1 orange
1 tbsp Grand Marnier or Cointreau (optional)

1 Pour the milk and cream into a saucepan and add the vanilla pod and orange zest. Bring to the boil.
2 Beat the egg yolks and sugar together in a bowl. Sit the bowl over a pan of simmering water and whisk in the boiled milk and cream. Stir until the mix coats the back of a spoon. Add the Grand Marnier or Cointreau if using.
3 Strain through a sieve into a jug and serve warm or cold. To prevent a skin forming, cover with greaseproof paper while cooling.

delicious contrasts

serves 4

watercress, spinach and parmesan salad
with mustard dressing

crispy duck breasts
with cabbage, bacon and onion and sautéed wild mushrooms

open apple pie

This menu shows how you can successfully bring together a variety of different tastes and textures. The crisp watercress and spinach salad provides a crunchy, peppery starter in contrast to the succulent duck breasts of the main course. As a fruity finale, open apple pie is topped with luscious caramel.

Shopping list

2 bunches of watercress
85g (3oz) baby spinach leaves
2 onions
1 small Savoy cabbage
350g (12oz) mixed wild mushrooms
8 Granny Smith apples
4 boneless duck breasts
8 rashers of streaky bacon
85g (3oz) parmesan cheese
2 eggs
unsalted butter
Cumberland sauce (see page 40)
crème fraîche or vanilla ice-cream
cider vinegar
caster sugar
Dijon mustard
300ml (10fl oz) groundnut oil
vegetable or olive oil
4 tsp clear honey
175g (6oz) sweet shortcrust pasty
(see page 8, 'variations')
icing sugar
soft, light brown sugar
285g jar apple purée or apple sauce

Prepare ahead

The day before

Bake the pastry discs and stack the apple towers for the pressed open apple pie

On the day

1 hour before guests arrive

Score the duck breasts ready for frying

Prepare the salad and chill

Mix the salad dressing and shave the parmesan, then chill

30 minutes before guests arrive

Blanch the cabbage, cool and drain, and set aside

Cook the duck and leave to rest

Just before sitting down to eat

Assemble the salad starter

Between the starter and main course

Fry the bacon, onion and cabbage

Sauté the mushrooms

Assemble the main course

Between the main course and pudding

Warm the apple towers in the microwave or oven

Arrange the apple towers on the pastry bases and caramelize the tops

watercress, spinach and parmesan salad

This is a light starter with crunchy watercress and spinach leaves tossed lightly in a mustard vinaigrette made with cider vinegar. Shaved parmesan provides a rich contrast.

you will need

preparation time
10 minutes

2 bunches of watercress, washed, shaken dry and stalks trimmed

85g (3oz) baby spinach leaves, washed, shaken dry and stalks trimmed
85g (3oz) parmesan, flaked or 40g (1½oz) freshly grated parmesan

for the mustard dressing
1½ tbsp cider vinegar
1 heaped tsp caster sugar
1 egg plus 1 egg yolk
2 tsp Dijon mustard
300ml (10fl oz) groundnut oil
salt and pepper

mixing the mustard dressing
1 Warm the sugar in the vinegar until it dissolves; leave to cool.
2 Mix the egg and egg yolk with the mustard and whisk in the sweetened vinegar.
3 Gradually dribble in the groundnut oil, whisking all the time. Season with salt and pepper.

tossing the salad
1 Place the watercress and baby spinach leaves in a large salad bowl.
2 Sprinkle the mustard dressing over the mixed salad leaves and toss thoroughly. Scatter the parmesan on top.
3 Serve the salad either in a large bowl so everyone can help themselves or arrange on individual plates.

crispy duck breasts
on a bed of cabbage, bacon and onion

These tender, duck breasts have a doubly-crisped skin – first pan-fried, then glazed with honey and roasted. The contrast between crunchy skin and juicy meat is a delight, especially served with tasty wild mushrooms and zesty Cumberland sauce.

you will need

preparation time	15 minutes
cooking time	35 minutes

for the duck

4 boneless duck breasts
1 tbsp vegetable or olive oil
25g (1oz) butter
8 rashers of streaky bacon
2 onions, sliced
1 small Savoy cabbage, quartered and shredded
salt and pepper
4 tsp clear honey

for the mushrooms

350g (12 oz) of wild mushrooms or a mixture of chestnut, portobello, shiitake and oyster.
knob of butter

cooking the duck

1 Pre-heat the oven to 220°C/425°F/gas 7.
2 Score the skin of the duck breasts quite heavily with a sharp knife. Leave only 5mm (¼in) between each scoring line to end up with a criss-cross pattern across the breast. Be careful to score only through the fat and not to cut into the flesh. Season.
3 Heat some oil in a roasting tin on top of the stove. Lay the duck breasts, skin side down, in the hot oil – be prepared for it to spit a little. Once the breasts are cooking swiftly, turn the heat down to medium and continue to cook until the skin is well browned and almost burnt.
4 Turn the breasts over to seal them, then finish cooking in the oven for 6-10 minutes. When cooked, the skin will look dark and crispy.

Recipe option

Cumberland sauce
makes 425ml (15fl oz)

rind and juice of 1 lemon
rind and juice of 1 orange
280g (10oz) redcurrant jelly
4 tbsp port
½ tsp ground ginger
½ tsp dry mustard
½ tsp arrowroot

5 Meanwhile, cut the bacon into 2.5cm (1in) pieces. Heat the butter in a pan and fry the bacon until browned. Add the onions and fry for 2-3 minutes. Add the cabbage with 1 tbsp water and fry for 2-3 minutes, then season.
6 Remove the duck breasts from the oven, spread 1 tsp honey on top of each breast and glaze under a hot grill. Let the duck breasts rest in a warm place for 5-10 minutes.

cooking the mushrooms

1 Wipe the mushrooms with a damp cloth to remove the grit and dirt. Leave the small mushrooms whole and chop the larger ones roughly.
2 Heat a knob of butter in a large frying-pan and add the mushrooms. Fry for 5-8 minutes; season lightly.

to serve

Pile a small mound of the cabbage, bacon and onion medley on each plate and put a duck breast on top. Serve with the mushrooms and sauce, if liked (see below).

1 Pare the rind from the lemon and orange in thin strips; blanch for 5 minutes in boiling water to reduce bitterness.
2 Heat the redcurrant jelly in a pan. When the jelly has melted, add the lemon and orange juice, port, ginger and mustard and simmer for 2-3 minutes.
3 Add the blanched orange and lemon peel and the arrowroot, and cook very briefly to allow the sauce to thicken. Serve cold.

open apple pie

This is a neat twist on a classic apple pie. The pastry is baked separately, then layers of apple slices and apple purée are stacked on top, dusted with sugar and caramelized under the grill. Crème fraîche or ice-cream adds a final flourish.

you will need

preparation time *30 minutes*

cooking time *30 minutes*

175g (6oz) sweet shortcrust pastry (see page 8, 'variations')

8 Granny Smith apples, peeled and cored

knob of butter

1 tbsp soft, light brown sugar

285g jar apple purée or smooth apple sauce

2-3 tbsp icing sugar to sift on top

crème fraîche or vanilla ice-cream, to serve

baking the pastry bases

1 Pre-heat the oven to 190°C/ 375°F/gas 5.

2 Roll out the pastry thinly and rest it in the fridge for 10 minutes. Using 8 ring moulds of 8cm (3¼in), cut out 8 discs of pastry.

3 Bake the pastry discs on greaseproof paper for 10-15 minutes. To keep them completely flat, place another sheet of greaseproof paper and a baking tray on top while baking. Take out of the oven and remove the top baking tray. Leave the pastry discs to cool and then remove them from the ring moulds.

preparing the apple stacks

1 Cut the apples into very thin rings. Heat the butter in a frying-pan and fry the apples quickly on both sides, a few at a time, until they are slightly browned and beginning to soften – don't let them get too soft or they will be difficult to handle.

2 When all the apple rings have been browned, melt a little more butter in the pan and return all the apple rings to it. Carefully turn the rings in the butter, then sprinkle over the sugar and heat until it caramelizes. Add 2 tsp water if all the apples are not completely caramelized. Leave to cool.

3 Grease the ring moulds and stack 3 apple slices in each. Spread ½ tsp apple purée over the surface, then add another 2 apple slices and another layer of purée. Continue layering until the ring is filled to the top, finishing with a film of purée. Cover the rings with plastic wrap, put a weight on top of each and chill.

assembling the open pies

1 Warm the apple stacks, either in a moderate oven for 10 minutes or briefly in a microwave, and sit them on the pastry discs.

2 To finish, dust the tops with icing sugar and glaze under the grill. Serve 1 pie per person, with a dollop of crème fraîche or ice-cream. The extra pies can be used as seconds or saved for another day.

home comforts

serves 4

spinach soup

crusty mustard pork chops
with mashed potatoes and Savoy cabbage

sticky fig tarts

When you have a few friends staying for the weekend or over the holidays, a simple yet delicious menu that doesn't take too long to prepare or serve is a blessing. Here everyone can enjoy a relaxing and satisfying dinner of spinach soup, pork chops cooked to perfection with a crisp mustard crust, followed by sticky fig tarts.

Shopping list

250g (9oz) spinach
800g (1lb 12oz) potatoes
1kg (2lb 4oz) Savoy cabbage
1 small onion
1 shallot
fresh parsley
fresh sage
5cm (2in) piece of fresh root ginger
6 fresh figs
4 x 175-225g (6-8oz) pork chops
225g (8oz) butter
100ml (3½fl oz) milk or single cream
4 tbsp single cream or natural Greek yoghurt
clotted cream
4 slices medium sliced white bread
140g (5oz) puff pastry (see page 9)
900ml (1½ pints) chicken stock (see page 10)
Dijon mustard
140g (5oz) soft, light brown sugar
olive oil
cooking oil

Prepare ahead

The day before

Make the spinach soup, cool and refrigerate

Make the ginger strips and store in an airtight container

On the day

2-3 hours before guests arrive

Make the breadcrumb topping for the pork chops and refrigerate

Make the fig tarts, but do not turn them out

Prepare the cabbage, rinse and keep in the fridge

Just before sitting down to eat

Grill the pork chops, cover with foil and set aside

Put the potatoes on to boil

Reheat and garnish the soup

Between the starter and main course

Drain and mash the potatoes

Cook the cabbage

Press the breadcrumb topping on to the chops and brown under the grill

Between the main course and pudding

Gently warm the base of the tart tins and turn out the fig tarts

spinach soup

This dark green, flavoursome soup is attractively garnished with a swirl of cream and crisp-fried ginger.

you will need

preparation time
10 minutes

cooking time
45 minutes

for the soup
250g (9oz) fresh leaf spinach, sorted, rinsed and well drained
1 small onion, finely chopped
25g (1oz) butter
1 tbsp olive oil
140g (5oz) potatoes, peeled and diced
900ml (1½ pints) hot chicken stock (see page 10)
salt and pepper

to garnish
4 tbsp single cream or natural Greek yogurt
5cm (2in) piece of fresh root ginger
cooking oil

1 In a large saucepan, fry the onion in the butter and oil for 5 minutes or until translucent, taking care not to let it brown. Add the potato and cook for another 5 minutes.
2 Add the spinach and cook for 3-4 minutes, stirring. Pour on the hot stock and bring to the boil. Simmer for 25 minutes, half-covered. Season to taste with salt and pepper. Leave to cool slightly before blitzing in a food processor or with a hand-blender.

garnishing the soup

1 Peel the ginger and cut lengthways into thin slices. Cut each slice into thin strips and blanch in boiling water. Pat dry with kitchen paper. Deep fry in oil at 180°C/350°F/gas 4 for 10 seconds, and drain.
2 Reheat the soup and pour into individual bowls. Swirl 1 tbsp cream or yoghurt into each bowl and top with the crispy ginger.

crusty mustard pork chops
with mashed potatoes and Savoy cabbage

A crisp herb and breadcrumb crust conceals tender pork chops. The meat is rich, so you need simple accompaniments only – creamy mashed potatoes and buttery Savoy cabbage are ideal. As an alternative, try red cabbage and apple instead of Savoy cabbage.

Cook's notes

Traditionally, sage and parsley are the herbs used in a stuffing for roast pork. The potent flavour of the sage is a good foil for the mild fattiness of the pork. For a less familiar taste experience, you can use 1 tsp chopped fresh tarragon instead of the sage and parsley – it goes particularly well with the Dijon mustard.

you will need

preparation time 15 minutes
cooking time 15 minutes for the chops; 20 minutes for the potatoes; 5 minutes for the cabbage

for the crusty mustard pork chops
4 x 175-225g (6-8oz) pork chops
4 slices white bread, crusts removed
salt and pepper
2 tbsp cooking oil
15g (½oz) butter
1 shallot, finely chopped
½ tsp chopped fresh parsley
½ tsp chopped fresh sage
1 dessertspoon Dijon mustard

for the mashed potato
650g (1lb 7oz) potatoes, peeled
55g (2oz) butter
100ml (3½fl oz) milk or single cream
salt and pepper

for the Savoy cabbage
1kg (2lb 4oz) Savoy cabbage, outer leaves and core removed
40g (1½oz) butter
salt and pepper

grilling the pork chops
1 Pre-heat the grill to medium.
2 Roughly tear the bread slices into a food processor or blender and whizz to make breadcrumbs.
3 Season the pork chops with salt and pepper and drizzle with oil. Grill for 5 minutes on each side.
4 Melt the butter in a frying-pan and cook the shallot for 2-3 minutes or until soft. Set aside to cool.
5 Combine the breadcrumbs, herbs and mustard in a bowl.
6 Once the shallot is cooled, stir into the breadcrumb mixture. Top the grilled chops with the mixture and place under a hot grill for 2-3 minutes until the crumbs are crisp and golden.

mashing the potatoes
1 Put the potatoes in a pan of boiling salted water and cook for 15-20 minutes or until tender.
2 Drain the potatoes, add the butter and milk or cream a little at a time and mash until smooth. Season with salt and pepper.

cooking the Savoy cabbage
1 Finely shred the cabbage, then rinse and drain.
2 Bring a pan of salted water to the boil, add the cabbage and cook for 2-3 minutes or until softened. Drain, toss in the butter and season with salt and pepper.

Recipe option

red cabbage and apple

1 red cabbage, finely shredded
2 tbsp brown sugar
2 Cox's apples, sliced
5 tbsp cider vinegar
55g (2oz) butter
salt and pepper

1 Simmer the cabbage, sugar and apples with 2 tbsp water in a pan with the lid on for 1 hour.
2 Stir in the cider vinegar and butter. Season with salt and pepper and cook, covered, for a further 10 minutes until tender.

Tip For an extra buttery caramel to spoon over the tarts, melt the remaining 55g (2oz) of butter with the rest of the soft, light brown sugar to form a silky, golden syrup. Trickle it over and around the tarts.

sticky fig tarts

Fresh figs are first softened in butter and then cooked in the style of a tarte tatin with a puff pastry top. Turn these delicious, caramelized sticky fig upside-down tarts out when ready. If you don't have four small tartlet tins, make one 20cm (8in) tart instead.

you will need

preparation time *30 minutes*

cooking time *50 minutes*

140g (5oz) puff pastry (see page 9)
6 fresh figs, halved lengthways
140g (5oz) soft, light brown sugar
85g (3oz) butter
clotted cream, to serve

1 Pre-heat the oven to 200°C/400°F/gas 6. Butter four 10cm (4in) diameter tartlet tins. It is important that the moulds are well buttered to prevent the figs from sticking and also to help the sugar to caramelize. Sprinkle 15g (½oz) of the sugar in each tin.

2 Melt 15g (½oz) butter in a frying-pan. Cook half the figs, cut side down, very quickly on a high heat until golden brown. Remove from the pan. Arrange three pieces, cut side down and points facing towards the centre, in two of the tartlet tins.

3 Melt another 15g (½oz) of butter and shallow-fry the remaining figs. Fill the other two tartlet tins.

4 Roll out the puff pastry thinly and cut out four 10cm (4in) circles. Sit a pastry circle on top of the fruit in each tartlet tin and bake for 20 minutes.

5 Once baked, remove from the oven and leave to rest for 5-6 minutes so the tarts are not too fragile when turned out.

6 Warm the base of the tins on the hob and turn the tarts out. Serve each tart with a good dollop of clotted cream.

prepared in advance

serves 4

gnocchi tartare
with tomato sauce and parmesan

pork stew
with potato and celeriac dauphinoise
and broccoli

maple syrup and
pecan nut ice-cream

Since time seems to be in short supply for most of us, this menu is planned so that you can make and freeze most of the first two courses in advance. When the gnocchi are defrosted, they just need 10 minutes in the frying-pan, while the pork stew simply needs reheating. For dessert, what could be easier than a delicious ice-cream dish!

Shopping list

900g (2lb) floury potatoes
450g (1lb) waxy potatoes
450g (1lb) broccoli
1 large celeriac
6 tomatoes
2 large onions
225g (8oz) button onions
600g (1lb 5oz) shallots
8 garlic cloves
225g (8oz) button mushrooms
bunch fresh tarragon plus 1 bouquet garni
225g (8oz) unsalted butter
1 litre (1¾ pints) double cream
300ml (10fl oz) milk
parmesan
6 eggs
1.3kg (3lb) pigs' cheeks or lean pork
25g (1oz) beef dripping or lard
225g (8oz) bacon rind
175g (6oz) smoked bacon
600ml (1 pint) chicken stock (see page 10)
capers
nutmeg
black peppercorns
175g (6oz) plain flour
sweet biscuits to serve with ice-cream
5 tbsp olive oil
vanilla essence
175g (6oz) maple syrup
85-115g (3-4oz) pecan nuts
1 bottle red wine

Prepare ahead

Up to a week in advance

Make the pork stew, cool and freeze

Make the potato and celeriac dauphinoise, cool and freeze

Make the gnocchi tartare and poach for 3-4 minutes. Allow to cool, then freeze

The evening before

Make the ice-cream and freeze

Take the stew and dauphinoise from the freezer to defrost, covered, at room temperature; take the gnocchi out of the freezer to defrost in the fridge

Make the tomato sauce and refrigerate

On the day

15 minutes before sitting down to eat

Put the dauphinoise in pre-heated oven to reheat

Begin reheating the pork stew

Heat the butter in a frying-pan and fry the gnocchi until golden and crisp

Reheat the tomato sauce

Toss the gnocchi with grated parmesan

Between the starter and main course

Transfer the ice-cream to the fridge to soften slightly

Finish the dauphinoise under the grill, cook the broccoli

Make sure the stew is piping hot

Between the main course and pudding

Scoop out the ice-cream

Garnish with pecan nuts and maple syrup

3 Add the flour, remaining oil, egg yolks, cooked shallots, capers and tarragon to the potato and mix. Season with salt, pepper and a touch of nutmeg.
4 On a floured surface, roll the mix into 1-2cm (½-¾in) balls. Poach the gnocchi in batches in a large pan of boiling salted water for 3-4 minutes. Leave them to cool on a tray covered with a clean cloth; place them so they don't touch each other.
5 When completely cool, put the tray in the freezer. After 2 hours, put the frozen gnocchi into an airtight container and return to the freezer.

making the sauce
1 Dunk the tomatoes in a pan of boiling water; skin, de-seed and chop into 5mm (¼in) dice.
2 In a frying-pan, heat 1 tbsp of oil with the garlic. Add the tomatoes and cook until very soft, allowing the liquid to evaporate. Season and add the remaining oil.
3 Leave to cool completely. Store in an airtight container in the fridge.

gnocchi tartare
with tomato sauce and parmesan

Gnocchi are Italian-style potato dumplings. Here, they're pepped up with piquant herbs and capers – hence 'tartare'. They're first poached, then fried until golden and tossed in parmesan cheese.

you will need
preparation time 1 hour
cooking time 5-10 minutes

for the gnocchi
900g (2lb) floury potatoes
1½ heaped tbsp finely chopped shallots
2 tbsp olive oil
115g (4oz) plain flour
2 egg yolks
1½ tbsp chopped capers

2 tsp chopped fresh tarragon
salt and pepper
grated nutmeg
grated parmesan
25g (1oz) butter for frying

for the tomato sauce
6 tomatoes
3 tbsp olive oil
garlic clove, crushed
salt and pepper

making the gnocchi
1 Cook the potatoes whole in boiling salted water until tender. Cool a little, peel and mash by pushing through a sieve or potato ricer.
2 Cook the shallots gently in 1½ tbsp of the oil – they should be soft but not coloured. Allow them to cool.

to serve
1 When the gnocchi are thawed – they should be taken out of the freezer at least 2 hours before serving – heat the butter in a large frying-pan and fry until crisp.
2 Reheat the tomato sauce. Toss the hot gnocchi with grated parmesan and serve with the tomato sauce. Garnish with tarragon.

pork stew
with potato and celeriac dauphinoise and broccoli

This tasty stew uses pigs' cheeks, an unusual cut of meat that you may need to order from the butcher. You just want the meaty part of the cheek. This is a classic recipe for stewing cheeks but if these are unavailable, replace with large chunks of lean pork.

you will need

preparation time *30 minutes for the pork; 15 minutes for the dauphinoise*
cooking time *1½-2 hours for the pork; 45-60 minutes for the dauphinoise; 8-10 minutes for the broccoli*

for the stew
1.3kg (3lb) pigs' cheeks, trimmed, or lean pork, cut into large chunks
salt and pepper
55g (2oz) plain flour
25g (1oz) beef dripping or lard
450g (1lb) shallots, sliced
225g (8oz) bacon rind, cut into strips
6 garlic cloves, halved
a few black peppercorns
1 bottle red wine
600ml (1 pint) chicken stock (see page 10)
1 bouquet garni
225g (8oz) button onions
115g (4oz) unsalted butter
175g (6oz) smoked bacon, rinded and cut into strips
225g (8oz) button mushrooms

for the dauphinoise
2 large onions, sliced
55g (2oz) unsalted butter
600ml (1 pint) double cream
1 garlic clove, crushed
salt and pepper
450g (1lb) waxy potatoes, thinly sliced
1 celeriac, peeled and thinly sliced

for the broccoli
450g (1lb) broccoli
knob of butter
salt and pepper

making the stew
1 Season the meat with salt and pepper; dip in flour to coat lightly.
2 Heat the lard or dripping in a frying-pan, fry the meat until coloured all over and transfer to a large flameproof casserole dish.
3 Fry the shallots in the same pan until tender. Transfer to casserole.
4 Fry the bacon rind for a few minutes and put this in the casserole.
5 Add the garlic, peppercorns, wine and stock to the pan, bring to a simmer, and pour over meat. Drop the bouquet garni into the casserole, cover and cook gently for 1½-2 hours until the meat is tender.

6 Meanwhile, fry the button onions in butter until softened. Add the bacon and mushrooms and fry for 2-3 minutes. Put in colander to drain.
7 Remove the meat from the casserole and strain the sauce through a sieve. Boil until it is reduced by ⅓-½, skimming if necessary. Add the meat to the drained onion and mushroom mix. Cool completely and freeze.

making the dauphinoise
1 Pre-heat the oven to 180°C/350°F/gas 4. Cook the onions in half the butter for 2-3 minutes, without colouring, and cool.
2 Bring the cream to the boil with the crushed garlic and remaining butter. Season with salt and pepper.
3 Arrange the onions, potatoes and celeriac in layers in a large ovenproof dish, making sure potatoes are on the top and bottom.
4 Pour on the cream and bake for 45-60 minutes until the vegetables are tender and have absorbed the cream. Cool completely and freeze.

cooking the broccoli
Trim broccoli and cut into florets. Steam for 8-10 minutes until tender. Toss with butter and season.

to serve
1 Defrost the stew and dauphinoise at room temperature for 24 hours.
2 Reheat the stew on the stove. Bring it slowly to a simmer and cook for 20-30 minutes until piping hot.
3 Reheat the dauphinoise at 190°C/375°F/gas 5 for about 30 minutes, finishing under the grill.

Tip If using an ice-cream maker, make sure you add the nuts to the ice-cream towards the end of churning or they will break down and discolour the mixture.

maple syrup and pecan nut ice-cream

The partnership of syrup and nuts is fantastic, the smooth sweetness blending well with the crunchy nuts. Serve this scrumptious dessert with sweet biscuits.

you will need

preparation time *1 hour*

freezing time *2-12 hours*

300ml (10fl oz) milk

300ml (10fl oz) double cream

few drops vanilla essence

4 egg yolks

175g (6oz) maple syrup

85-115g (3-4oz) pecan nuts, chopped

sweet biscuits, to serve

1 Mix the milk, cream and vanilla essence in a pan. Bring to the boil.
2 While the cream mix is heating, beat the egg yolks with 115g (4oz) of the maple syrup until thick and pale, using an electric mixer.
3 Pour the hot cream mixture into the egg and maple syrup mixture, stirring all the time until well blended. Return to the heat and cook, stirring until the mixture coats the back of the spoon. Do not allow to boil. Leave to cool.
4 Stir in the remaining maple syrup.

If you are not using an ice-cream maker, add the nuts at this point too, reserving a few for decoration. Turn the mix into a freezer tray or bowl and freeze, stirring regularly until set.
5 If you are using an ice-cream maker, churn the mixture in it for 20 minutes, by which time it will have thickened and increased in volume.
6 Reserve a few pecan nuts for decoration and add the rest to the ice-cream. Churn for a further 10 minutes. Don't let the ice-cream freeze completely in the machine or it will be over-churned and slightly grainy. Take it out when thick and starting to freeze and put in the freezer.
7 Keep the ice-cream in the freezer for up to 24 hours. Transfer it to the fridge 30 minutes before serving to soften a little. Garnish with pecan nuts and extra maple syrup, and serve with the ready-made biscuits.

classics with a twist

serves 4

iced melon salad

lamb and black pudding roll
with roast new potatoes and
buttered spinach

roast plums in port
with almond meringue biscuits

If you have time, it's fun to make something unusual and impressive with well-known ingredients – like rolling a rack of lamb around black pudding for the main course. Equally snazzy are iced melon salad for starters and the roast plums in port with almond meringue biscuits for dessert.

Shopping list

½ cucumber
675g (1½lb) spinach
450g (1lb) new potatoes
2 bunches watercress
bag of rocket leaves
1 small charentais or cantaloupe melon
1 lemon
12 plums
2 boned racks of lamb with 6-8 cutlets each
15-20cm (6-8in) black pudding, 2.5-3cm
(1-1¼in) in diameter
4 eggs
85g (3oz) butter
142ml carton clotted cream
150ml (5fl oz) beef consommé or stock
(see page 9)
French bread
115g (4oz) toasted almonds
175g (6oz) caster sugar
25g (1oz) plain flour
2 tsp cornflour
5 tbsp olive oil
2 tsp coarse sea salt
2 tsp wholegrain mustard
1 tbsp white wine vinegar
4 tbsp walnut oil
4 tbsp sunflower or groundnut oil
½ bottle red wine
200ml (7fl oz) port

Prepare ahead

The day before
Roll and tie the lamb and black pudding and refrigerate
Make the almond meringue biscuits and store in an airtight container

On the day
In the morning
Prepare the melon and cucumber for the starter and make the mustard dressing
Roast the plums and make the port syrup

1 hour before sitting down to eat
Wash and prepare the leaves for the salad
Mix the olive oil and lemon dressing
Wash the potatoes and spinach

15 minutes before sitting down to eat
Put the potatoes in to roast
Assemble and dress the salad starter
Put the lamb in to roast

Between the starter and main course
Make the red-wine sauce
Cook the spinach
Carve the lamb and black pudding roll into slices

Between the main course and pudding
Gently warm the roast plums in their syrup

Tip You can use other kinds of melon – or a mixture of melons – if you like, although you'll probably need to use just half of a larger one, such as a ripe honeydew or galia.

Mix the walnut and sunflower oils together and pour very slowly into the mustard mixture, whisking vigorously all the time. Season and set aside.

3 Peel and halve the cucumber and scoop out the seeds. Cut into rough 1cm (½in) dice, sprinkle with a little salt and refrigerate until needed. Tear the watercress into sprigs.

4 When ready to serve, transfer the melon, cucumber, rocket and watercress to a salad bowl. Whisk together the olive oil and lemon juice and season to taste. Pour a little over the salad and spoon on about half the mustard dressing. Toss together until the melon and salad leaves are well coated.

to serve
Transfer portions to individual plates and drizzle with the remaining mustard dressing and lemony olive oil. Serve with plenty of warm crusty French bread to soak up the dressings.

iced melon salad

This recipe uses sweet charentais or cantaloupe melons for their striking orange flesh. For a cool and very refreshing salad, keep the melon chilled right up until the moment you serve it.

you will need

preparation time
30 minutes

chilling time
at least 30 minutes

1 small charentais or cantaloupe melon
2 tsp wholegrain mustard
1 egg yolk
1 tbsp white wine vinegar
4 tbsp walnut oil

2 tbsp sunflower or groundnut oil
salt and pepper
½ cucumber
2 bunches watercress, washed and drained
bag rocket leaves, washed and drained
2 tbsp olive oil
squeeze of lemon juice
warm crusty French bread, to serve

1 Quarter the melon and scoop out the seeds. Prepare it on a plate so that you can catch any juice. Remove the skin and cut the flesh into rough 2.5cm (1in) dice. Put the melon and juice in a bowl and refrigerate for at least 30 minutes.

2 Whisk the mustard, egg yolk and vinegar together.

lamb and black pudding roll
with roast new potatoes and buttered spinach

Simple ingredients excel in this wonderful dinner-party dish – the striking combination of tender lamb and flavoursome black pudding can't fail to delight. It's served with a rich red-wine sauce, roast new potatoes and lightly cooked buttered spinach.

Cook's notes

If your butcher is boning the racks of lamb for you, ask him to leave the skin and fat on for this recipe so that you have at least a 10cm (4in) flap of skin to wrap around the black pudding. You will have to trim off most of the fat yourself so that the skin and fat together are no more than 3mm (⅛in) thick.

you will need

preparation time *45 minutes*

cooking time *30 minutes*

for the lamb and black pudding roll
2 racks of lamb with 6-8 cutlets each, boned and trimmed (see 'Cook's notes' above)
15-20cm (6-8in) black pudding, with a diameter of 2.5-3cm (1-1½in)
salt and pepper
2 tbsp sunflower or groundnut oil
½ bottle red wine
150ml (5fl oz) beef consommé or stock (see page 9)
2 tsp cornflour mixed to a paste with 2 tsp consommé or stock (see page 9)

for the roast new potatoes
450g (1lb) new potatoes
3 tbsp olive oil
2 tsp coarse sea salt

for the buttered spinach
675g (1½lb) spinach, washed
40g (1½oz) butter
salt and pepper

preparing the roll

1 Cut the black pudding in half lengthways and pull off the skin. Take one rack of lamb and lay one half of black pudding along the skin so that the cut side is touching the meat. Season with pepper.

2 Fold the skin over the lamb and pudding to form a cylinder. Tie the roll securely with cooking twine and wrap tightly in plastic wrap. Repeat with the other rack of lamb and remaining black pudding. Refrigerate for a few hours to firm up (preferably overnight).

roasting the meat and potatoes

1 Pre-heat the oven to 200°C/400°F/gas 6.

2 Put the potatoes in a roasting tin and toss with the oil and salt. Roast for 25-30 minutes until browned and cooked through.

3 While the potatoes are in the oven, place a roasting tin over moderate heat and add the oil. Brown the lamb joints until coloured all over. Roast for 15-18 minutes for medium-done meat.

making the red-wine sauce

1 Once the meat has roasted, set it aside to rest for about 10 minutes.

2 Drain the excess fat from the roasting tin. Pour in the red wine and bring to the boil over moderate heat, stirring in any crusty bits. Boil until reduced by a half.

3 Add the consommé or stock and bring back to a simmer. Stir in the cornflour paste and cook until slightly thickened. Season to taste, strain and keep the sauce warm during carving.

cooking the spinach

1 Melt the butter in a large saucepan and stir in the spinach, with the washing water still clinging to the leaves.

2 When the leaves have wilted, drain off surplus water and season. Serve immediately.

to serve

Remove the cooking twine and carve each rack into six slices – three per portion. Spoon over the sauce and add the potatoes and spinach.

Tip For an extra rich and creamy pudding, top the plums with clotted cream after pouring on the port syrup. It tastes fantastic!

baking the biscuits

1 Pre-heat the oven to 150°C/300°F/gas 2. Line a baking tray with a sheet of non-stick baking parchment.
2 Grind 85g (3oz) almonds in a food mill. Chop the rest of the nuts.
3 Whisk the egg whites and sugar together until stiff, and gently fold in the flour. Add the ground nuts and butter and mix well.
4 Transfer the mixture to a piping bag fitted with a plain 1cm (½in) nozzle. Pipe finger shapes about 7.5cm (3in) long on the baking tray. Sprinkle each biscuit with the chopped nuts. Bake for 30 minutes, then cool.

stewing the plums

1 Turn the oven up to 200°C/400°F/gas 6.
2 Melt the butter in an ovenproof frying-pan and fry the plums for a few minutes until they begin to colour. Transfer the pan to the oven and cook for 10-15 minutes.
3 Take the pan out of the oven and place it over medium heat. Sprinkle over the sugar. As the plums starts to caramelize, roll them so they are coated in the syrup. Add the port, bring to the boil and reduce by a third.

to serve

Spoon the plums into small bowls, and pour on some port syrup. Serve with the biscuits. Store any leftover biscuits in an airtight container.

roast plums in port

A delightfully easy dessert – these plums are served in a rich port sauce with almond meringue biscuits.

you will need
preparation time *25 minutes*
cooking time *45 minutes*

for the almond meringue biscuits (makes 24)
115g (4oz) toasted almonds
4 egg whites
115g (4oz) caster sugar

25g (1oz) plain flour, sifted
15g (½oz) unsalted butter, melted

for the plums
12 plums
25g (1oz) butter
55g (2oz) caster sugar
200ml (7fl oz) port

winter warmer

serves 4

cream of onion soup

stewed venison in red wine
with bubble-and-squeak cakes
and cabbage

cranachan parfait

All the courses of this satisfying menu actually taste even better if they are prepared in advance. On the day, the venison stew should be warmed through slowly and the creamy onion soup gently reheated. Remove the cranachan parfait from the freezer a few minutes before serving.

Shopping list

275g (10oz) button onions
1.3kg (3lb) onions
1 garlic clove
7 celery sticks
3 carrots
6 open cup mushrooms
675g (1½lb) Brussels sprouts
1 small potato
675g (1½lb) mashed potatoes (see page 46)
1kg (2lb 4oz) Savoy cabbage
1 leek
fresh raspberries
fresh chives
fresh thyme
1 bay leaf
juniper berries and black peppercorns
175g (6oz) unsalted butter
350ml (12fl oz) double cream
4 eggs
900ml (1½ pints) chicken stock (see page 10)
900ml (1½ pints) beef stock (see page 9)
900g (2lb) haunch of venison
clear honey
115g (4oz) caster sugar
115g (4oz) medium oatmeal
1 bottle red wine
whisky
French bread or parmesan croûtons
(see page 63)

Prepare ahead

Two days before

Make the cranachan parfait
Marinate the venison overnight in the fridge

The day before

Make the onion soup (leaving out the cream), then liquidize, cool and keep in the fridge
Prepare and cook the venison stew, then cool and keep in the fridge overnight
Prepare the mashed potato bubble-and-squeak cakes and chill

On the day

During the morning

Fry the bubble-and-squeak cakes and transfer to a baking tray
Shred and wash the cabbage

1 hour 15 minutes before sitting down to eat

Warm the venison stew

Just before sitting down to eat

Heat the onion soup and warm the French bread
Put the bubble-and-squeak cakes in the moderate oven to heat for 30 minutes

Between the starter and main course

Cook the cabbage for 2-3 minutes in lightly salted boiling water
Check the venison stew and finish warming on top of the stove if necessary
Take the cranachan parfait out of the freezer to soften slightly

cream of onion soup

For minimal preparation, cooking and cost, a bowl of onion soup makes a warming starter without being too filling. This starter tastes even better served with slices of warm French bread or parmesan croûtons.

you will need
preparation time *15 minutes*
cooking time *30 minutes*

675g (1½lb) onions, chopped
55g (2oz) unsalted butter
2-3 celery sticks, roughly diced
1 small potato, roughly diced
1 leek (white part only), diced

Recipe option
parmesan croûtons

2 thick slices of crustless bread, cut into 15mm (⅝in) squares
olive oil
parmesan

1 Pour enough oil into a roasting tin to cover the bottom. Drop in the bread and shake to coat.
2 Cook in a hot oven, turning every 1-2 minutes until golden brown.
3 When hot and crisp, sprinkle liberally with cheese.

1 small garlic clove, chopped
900ml (1½ pints) chicken stock (see page 10)
2 tbsp double cream
2 tbsp finely chopped chives
French bread or parmesan croutons (see 'Recipe option' above), to serve

1 Melt the butter in a pan. When it begins to froth, add all the vegetables and garlic and cook for 8-10 minutes over a medium heat without colouring.
2 Pour in the stock and bring to a simmer. Continue to cook for 20-30 minutes.
3 Blitz the soup to the preferred consistency. If necessary, use extra stock to thin it down. For a smoother soup, push it through a sieve.
4 Stir the cream into the hot soup at the last minute. Add the chives and serve with the bread or croûtons (see 'Recipe option' above).

stewed venison in red wine
with bubble-and-squeak cakes and cabbage

Venison is a lean meat with a distinctive taste which benefits from being cooked slowly in a rich wine sauce to keep it moist and tender. Crisp bubble-and-squeak cakes and Savoy cabbage complement its robust flavours.

you will need
preparation time *10 minutes plus at least 12 hours marinating*

cooking time *2 hours 25 minutes*

for the stew
900g (2lb) haunch of venison, cut into large chunks

2 tbsp vegetable oil

2 onions, sliced

900ml (1½ pints) beef stock (see page 9)

275g (10oz) button onions

3 carrots

4 celery sticks, sliced

6 open cup mushrooms, quartered

salt and pepper

for the marinade
2 onions, quartered

1 sprig of fresh thyme and 1 bay leaf

4 juniper berries, crushed

6 black peppercorns, crushed

1 bottle red wine (half for step 7)

for the bubble-and-squeak cakes
675g (1½lb) Brussels sprouts

55g (2oz) unsalted butter

2 large onions, thinly sliced

675g (1½lb) mashed potato (see 'mashing the potatoes' on page 46),

made without cream or milk

salt and pepper

for the Savoy cabbage
1kg (2lb 4oz) Savoy cabbage

40g (1½oz) butter

salt and pepper

making the stew
1 Mix the marinade ingredients together and stir in the venison chunks. Cover and leave to stand overnight or for at least 12 hours to tenderize. Drain off the liquid and reserve. Discard the other marinade ingredients.

2 Pat the venison chunks dry with kitchen paper. Heat 1 tbsp vegetable oil in a cast-iron casserole dish and brown the meat. When sealed all over, remove and set aside.

3 Add the 2 onions to the casserole dish and fry for 2-3 minutes. Add the marinating liquid and boil to reduce by half. Return the venison pieces to the casserole, pour in the stock and bring to a simmer.

4 Cover and cook gently for 1½-2 hours on top of the stove until the meat is tender, skimming fat from the surface occasionally.

5 Meanwhile, heat 1 tbsp vegetable oil in a frying-pan and fry the button onions. While they are softening, quarter the carrots lengthways and then cut into 2cm (¾in) pieces.

6 Remove the onions, add the carrots and celery and cook until they are lightly coloured. Set aside with the onions.

7 Fry the mushrooms for a few minutes. Return all the vegetables to the pan and cover with the remaining wine. Boil until nearly all the wine has evaporated, cooking the vegetables in the process.

8 Stir the vegetables into the meat and check the seasoning. Cool before storing in the fridge.

9 To serve, warm the stew at 170°C/325°F/gas 3 for 1 hour.

making the bubble-and-squeak cakes
1 Cook the sprouts in boiling salted water. Drain, then cool under cold-running water and drain again. Slice.

2 Melt half the butter in a frying-pan and cook the onions gently for 4-5 minutes until softened. Cool.

3 Mix the onions with the sprouts and add the potato, a spoonful at a time, so that the mixture has a firm texture. Add salt and pepper.

4 Melt the rest of the butter in a clean frying-pan. Press the mixture into ring moulds and, leaving the rings on, fry the cakes until crispy. Turn over and repeat. Keep any left over for the next day's breakfast.

cooking the Savoy cabbage
See page 46 for details on how to cook the cabbage.

Tip To toast the oatmeal, spread a thin layer over a baking tray and place it under a grill on a medium setting. Shake the tray frequently to turn the oatmeal. Toast until it's evenly and lightly browned.

cranachan parfait

Traditionally served in Scotland at Halloween, cranachan is a whipped cream, whisky and oatmeal dessert, sweetened with honey. Here this classic pudding is frozen into a smooth parfait and garnished with fresh raspberries and honeycomb.

you will need

preparation time *20 minutes*
freezing time *at least 24 hours*

4 egg yolks
115g (4oz) caster sugar
300ml (10fl oz) double cream
2 tsp clear honey
115g (4oz) medium oatmeal, lightly toasted (see 'Tip' above) and cooled
1-2 tbsp whisky to taste (optional)

to serve

clear honey
fresh raspberries

1 With a balloon whisk or electric hand mixer, whisk the egg yolks and sugar together in a bowl over a pan of warm water until the mixture is pale and thick.

2 Remove from the heat and continue to whisk while pouring in the cream until the mixture thickens. Fold in the honey, oatmeal and whisky, if liked.

3 Pour into four 150ml (5fl oz) moulds and freeze until firm. To unmould, dip the bases of the moulds in hot water and turn out on to plates. Serve with a drizzle of honey and fresh raspberries.

vegetarian treat

serves 4

fried halloumi
with sun-dried tomatoes and pine nuts

herb risotto
with a mozzarella glaze

iced lime soufflé
with Marsala biscuits

This enticing vegetarian menu mixes flavours to create a delicious and harmonious meal. Halloumi cheese is balanced by a mixture of leaves, nuts and tomatoes, while a rich, mellow risotto is topped with melting mozzarella. After these savoury dishes, the zingy lime dessert makes a superbly refreshing finale.

Shopping list

2 onions
2 garlic cloves
fresh thyme, chives, basil, tarragon and parsley
mixed salad leaves
5 limes
115g (4oz) unsalted butter
150ml (5fl oz) double cream
parmesan
55-85g (2-3oz) mozzarella
1 packet halloumi
4 eggs
175g (6oz) caster sugar
55g (2oz) golden syrup
55g (2oz) plain flour
ground ginger
225g (8oz) arborio rice
55g (2oz) pine nuts
900ml-1.2 litres (1½-2 pints) ready-made vegetable stock
dark chocolate
jar sun-dried tomatoes in oil
olive oil
25ml (1fl oz) balsamic vinegar
3 tbsp Marsala
crusty bread
8-12 even-sized rose or violet leaves

Prepare ahead

On the day

At least 3 hours before guests arrive

Make the lime soufflés and freeze
Make the chocolate leaves and refrigerate
Make the Marsala biscuits, cool and store in an airtight container

30 minutes before guests arrive

Cook the risotto, without adding the herbs or cheeses, and keep warm
Toast the pine nuts and prepare the balsamic dressing for the starter

10 minutes before sitting down to eat

Fry the halloumi. Arrange the salad on plates, top with the dressing and add the halloumi

Between the starter and main course

Add the herbs, parmesan and butter to the risotto. Top with mozzarella; grill and finish with olive oil and extra parmesan

Between the main course and pudding

Remove the soufflés from the freezer, decorate with lime zest and chocolate leaves and serve with biscuits

fried halloumi
with sun-dried tomatoes and pine nuts

Halloumi cheese is creamy, salty and succulent. Here it's balanced by peppery green leaves, sun-dried tomatoes, sweet pine nuts and a piquant balsamic vinaigrette dressing.

you will need

preparation time
15 minutes

cooking time *10 minutes*

for the salad
1 packet halloumi, thickly sliced
4-6 sun-dried tomatoes in oil, drained and finely chopped
55g (2oz) pine nuts

mixed salad leaves
olive oil, for frying
crusty bread, to serve

for the dressing
25ml (1fl oz) balsamic vinegar
1 garlic clove, finely chopped
salt and pepper
50ml (2fl oz) oil from the sun-dried tomatoes

1 Heat a large frying-pan. Add the pine nuts and toast at a low heat, tossing occasionally, for about 5 minutes until golden and fragrant. Set aside.
2 For the dressing, put the vinegar, garlic and seasoning in a bowl. Gradually add the oil, whisking as you do so. Set aside.

3 Arrange the mixed salad leaves on serving plates. Heat a little olive oil in a frying-pan and fry the halloumi slices for 3-4 minutes on each side, until golden brown. Keep the heat high to drive off moisture from the cheese.
4 Place the sun-dried tomatoes and toasted pine nuts on the salad leaves. Sprinkle the dressing over the top. Add the slices of fried halloumi, hot from the pan, and serve immediately with some crusty bread.

herb risotto
with a mozzarella glaze

Risotto is a classic Italian dish that is simple and versatile. Here, the thick savoury rice is laced with the flavours of fresh herbs as well as the classic tang of parmesan cheese. A sprinkling of mozzarella, added at the last minute and grilled, makes a sumptuous topping.

Tip The starter's Mediterranean tang calls for a robust wine: go for a full-bodied red Rioja Crianza or Reserva, matured in oak casks. With red Rioja, it's best to open the bottle a good hour before you drink it. Alternatively, be adventurous and try rich, dry white Rioja, well chilled. Both these wines also work well with risotto. The lime in the pudding will overpower most wines, but you could always sip a glass of port or madeira while finishing off the Marsala biscuits.

Cook's notes

To make authentic risotto, it's essential to use the right type of rice. Arborio rice contains lots of starch. During cooking, the rice grains absorb several times their own volume of liquid and release starch to introduce a thick, sticky consistency to the finished dish.

Make sure that the stock is at the same temperature as the rice when you add it. Cool stock lowers the temperature of the risotto and disrupts the cooking process. Keep the stock in a saucepan on the stove over a low heat and add it gradually.

Ensure that the heat under the risotto is very low too: the rice should be barely bubbling, no more. Stir frequently to ensure even absorption and help the rice release its starch.

you will need

preparation time 5 minutes

cooking time 25-30 minutes

55g (2oz) butter

2 onions, finely chopped

1 garlic clove, chopped

225g (8oz) arborio rice

900ml-1.2 litres (1½-2 pints) ready-made vegetable stock

2 tbsp grated parmesan, plus extra for sprinkling

salt and pepper

½ tsp each fresh chopped thyme and chives

2 tsp fresh chopped basil

1 tsp each fresh chopped tarragon and parsley

55-85g (2-3oz) mozzarella, coarsely grated

olive oil

1 Melt the butter in a frying-pan. Add the onions and garlic. Cook over a medium heat for a few minutes until the onions are soft but not brown.

2 Add the arborio rice and cook, stirring, for a minute or so until the grains become translucent and each one is coated in butter.

3 Heat the vegetable stock, then add a ladleful to the rice. Cook, stirring occasionally, until the liquid is completely absorbed; then add another ladleful. Keep adding the stock, a ladleful at a time, allowing the rice to absorb it before adding more. Stir frequently. Cook until the rice is *al dente*, which should take 20-25 minutes.

4 Stir in 2 tbsp parmesan and more butter, if necessary, to achieve a loose, creamy consistency. Season and stir in the chopped fresh herbs.

to serve

Spoon the risotto into bowls and top each portion with mozzarella. Place under a hot grill until the cheese is melted and beginning to turn golden; then trickle a little extra olive oil over the top to moisten it. Serve sprinkled with plenty of parmesan.

iced lime soufflé
with Marsala biscuits

This is not so much a soufflé as a frozen parfait served in individual glasses. The lacy biscuits are like brandy snaps – their crunch complements the smooth soufflé beautifully. Chocolate leaves give a stylish finish.

you will need
preparation time *30 minutes*

freezing time *at least 2 hours*

for the soufflé
juice and finely grated zest of 4 limes, plus extra zest to decorate

4 eggs, separated

115g (4oz) caster sugar

150ml (5fl oz) double cream, lightly whipped

2 tbsp Marsala

for the biscuits
55g (2oz) unsalted butter

55g (2oz) caster sugar

55g (2oz) golden syrup

55g (2oz) plain flour

a pinch of ground ginger

1 tbsp Marsala

1 tbsp lime juice

for the chocolate leaves
8-12 even-sized rose or violet leaves, washed thoroughly

chocolate, melted

making the soufflés
1 In a pan, boil the lime juice and zest to reduce by three-quarters. Cool.
2 Put the egg yolks, sugar and reduced lime juice in a heatproof bowl over a pan of simmering water. Whisk until the mixture is thick, light and at least doubled in volume.
3 Remove from the heat and continue to whisk until the mixture cools to room temperature. Fold in the cream and Marsala.
4 Whisk the egg whites until they form stiff peaks, and fold into the soufflé mix. Spoon the mix into glasses and leave to set in the freezer for at least 2 hours. Before serving, decorate with chocolate leaves and lime zest.

making the biscuits
1 Pre-heat the oven to 180°C/350°F/gas 4. Line 2 baking trays with baking parchment.
2 Put the butter, sugar and syrup in a heavy-based saucepan and heat gently until the sugar dissolves. Take off the heat and cool for 2-3 minutes.
3 Beat the flour and ginger into the sugar mixture. Add the Marsala and lime juice. Leave the mixture to cool.
4 Place teaspoons of the mix on the baking trays, setting them well apart to allow for spreading.
5 Bake for 7-10 minutes, until spread out and golden. Cool for 1 minute, then lift off the tray with a palette knife. Shape into curls by wrapping around a rolling pin, and cool on a wire rack.

making the chocolate leaves
1 Dry the leaves and brush the undersides with chocolate and leave in the fridge to set.
2 Carefully peel the leaves from the chocolate and chill until needed.

lunch to go

serves 4

roast mushroom soup

Caesar salad
with sun-dried tomato bread

plum and almond pizza
with lemon parmesan

This tasty menu can be served at home any day of the week, or even packed up and taken to a friend's house for an informal lunchtime get-together. A warming mushroom soup precedes a classic Caesar salad, and to finish a slice of plum and almond 'pizza' tart goes down a treat with a cup of freshly brewed coffee.

Shopping list

750g (1½lb) large flat mushrooms
fresh parsley or tarragon
6 little gem or 2 cos lettuces
2 onions
1 large potato
6 lemons
12-14 plums
1 garlic clove
600ml (1 pint) chicken stock (see page 10)
300ml (10fl oz) single cream
175g (6oz) unsalted butter
3 eggs
350g (12oz) sweet shortcrust pastry (see page 8, 'variations')
85g (3oz) grated parmesan
25g (1oz) flaked parmesan
4 thick slices wholemeal bread
sun-dried tomato bread
12 canned anchovy fillets
150-300ml (5-10fl oz) extra virgin olive oil
1-2 tbsp soft, light brown sugar
25g (1oz) plain flour
115g (4oz) caster sugar
85g (3oz) ground almonds
2 tsp capers
Worcestershire sauce
Dijon mustard
cooking oil
olive oil
Tabasco sauce

Prepare ahead

The day before

Make the mushroom soup, let it cool and keep it in the fridge overnight

Bake the plum pizza, leave to cool before wrapping in foil

Make the croûtons for the salad and store in an airtight container

Wash the lettuce for the salad and keep in the fridge overnight

Put the parmesan flakes and anchovy fillets for the salad in separate containers

Check the supply of cutlery, china and napkins (if taking it elsewhere)

Put the ice packs for the cool bag into the freezer if necessary

On the day

In the morning (if taking it elsewhere)

Reheat the soup and pour it into a thermos flask

Parboil the egg and use it to make the dressing for the salad; decant the dressing into a bottle

Pack a cool bag or box with the thermos, bread, croûtons, lettuce, parmesan, anchovies, salad dressing and plum pizza – add any napkins, cutlery and china you think you may need

Just before sitting down to eat

Mix the lettuce, croûtons, anchovies and parmesan flakes together and toss in the dressing

Slice the bread to serve with the soup and the salad

Tip If you decide to use tarragon for extra flavour, add a few leaves during cooking to enhance the taste. Adding a squeeze of lemon juice after liquidizing will bring out a rich mushroom flavour.

1 Pre-heat the oven to 220°C/425°F/gas 7.
2 Wipe rather than soak the mushrooms.
3 Heat a roasting tin or ovenproof frying-pan on the hob and add the cooking oil.
4 Season the mushrooms and add them to the pan. Fry on a high heat to colour them well. Once they are coloured on one side, turn them over to colour again. Then put them in the oven for 8-10 minutes.
5 Soften the onions and potato in butter, without colouring. Add the stock and bring to a simmer.
6 Roughly chop up the roasted mushrooms, saving one or two to use as garnish later. Add the rest to the stock – using a little stock to rinse any residue from the tin or pan.
7 Bring the soup back to a simmer and add the cream. Season with salt and pepper.
8 Cook for 5-6 minutes, then remove from the heat. Allow to cool a little before blitzing until smooth. Return to the pan and heat through again. When hot, serve at once, garnished with slices of mushroom, or pour into a large thermos if you are taking it elsewhere.

roast mushroom soup

Cream of mushroom soup is always a great favourite. Roasting the mushrooms before putting them in the soup intensifies their rich, earthy flavour.

you will need

preparation time
10 minutes

cooking time
30 minutes

750g (1½lb) large flat mushrooms

2 tbsp cooking oil
2 onions, finely chopped
1 large potato, peeled and cut into roughly 1cm (½in) cubes
knob of butter
600ml (1 pint) chicken stock (see page 10)

300ml (10fl oz) single cream
salt and pepper
chopped fresh parsley or tarragon to garnish (optional)

Caesar salad
with sun-dried tomato bread

One of the classics of world cuisine, this salad makes a quick and tasty light lunch. A delicious sun-dried tomato bread adds an extra flavour and is extremely good for soaking up the remainder of the dressing.

you will need

preparation time
15 minutes

cooking time
7-10 minutes

for the salad
6 little gem or 2 cos lettuces
8 canned anchovy fillets
4 thick slices wholemeal bread
olive oil
25g (1oz) grated parmesan
25g (1oz) flaked parmesan
sun-dried tomato bread

for the dressing
15g (½oz) anchovy fillets, drained and chopped
2 tsp capers
2 tsp Worcestershire sauce
½ tsp Dijon mustard
dash of Tabasco sauce
juice of ½ lemon
1 garlic clove, crushed
2 tbsp finely grated parmesan
1 egg, boiled for 1½ minutes only
150-300ml (5-10fl oz) extra virgin olive oil
salt and pepper

Watchpoint!

If you are serving the salad to anyone who is pregnant or elderly, you must not use an undercooked egg. An an alternative, use 1-2 hard-boiled yolks. Crumble them in with the dressing mix before you blitz all the ingredients in a liquidizer.

preparing the salad

1 Pre-heat the oven to 200°C/400°F/gas 6.
2 Break the little gems into separate leaves or cut the cos into pieces. Split the anchovy fillets into strips.
3 To make the croûtons, remove the crusts from the bread and cut the bread into 1cm (½in) squares. Put them in a single layer on a baking tray and sprinkle with olive oil.
4 Bake the bread cubes in the oven for 5-8 minutes, turning regularly until they are golden brown and crunchy. While the croûtons are still hot, toss them in a bowl of grated parmesan.

making the dressing

1 Place all the dressing ingredients in a liquidizer, using just 150ml (5fl oz) oil at first, and blitz until thick and creamy. Check the seasoning, going easy on the salt because of the saltiness of the anchovies.
2 For a smooth dressing, press it through a sieve; otherwise serve the dressing slightly chunky. To get the consistency thick enough to coat the back of a spoon, add more oil, a little at a time.
3 Keep the dressing in the fridge until ready to use, or pour it into a bottle to take elsewhere.

assembling the salad

1 Just before serving, toss the lettuce leaves in the dressing, making sure they are all well coated.
2 Add the anchovy strips, croûtons and flaked parmesan.
3 Serve with chunky slices of sun-dried tomato bread.

plum and almond pizza
with lemon parmesan

Your friends will love this fruity 'pizza' tart, which goes really well with coffee.

you will need
preparation time *25 minutes*
cooking time *20 minutes*

for the lemon parmesan
caster sugar to bind
zest of 4 lemons, finely grated

for the plums
knob of butter
12-14 plums, halved and stoned
1-2 tbsp soft, light brown sugar

for the base
350g (12oz) sweet shortcrust pastry (see page 8, 'variations')

for the frangipane filling
115g (4oz) unsalted butter
115g (4oz) caster sugar
2 eggs
85g (3oz) ground almonds
zest of 2 lemons, finely grated
juice of ½ lemon
25g (1oz) plain flour

making the lemon parmesan
1 Work enough caster sugar into the lemon zest to create granules.
2 Spread the granules on a baking tray and leave in a warm place for 24 hours. Store in a screw-top jar.

preparing the plums
1 Melt the butter in a frying-pan and put in the plums, cut side down. Increase the heat and fry until the edges are almost burnt. Add the sugar to caramelize the plums. (Don't let them soften too much.)
2 Add a little water to the pan to make a caramel sauce to coat the plums. Transfer the plums to a plate to cool. Pour off and save the syrup.

baking the base
1 Pre-heat the oven to 200°C/400°F/gas 6. Line a 25-30cm (10-12in) pizza tray with greaseproof paper.
2 Roll out the pastry thinly and use it to line the pizza tray. Do not trim the pastry to fit the tray at this stage.
3 Line the pastry with greaseproof paper and baking beans and bake in the oven for 5 minutes.
4 Remove from the oven (turn the oven down to 180°C/350°F/gas 4), and trim the pastry around the tray.

making the frangipane filling
1 Beat together the butter and sugar until pale and creamy. Mix in 1 egg at a time, sprinkling in a little ground almonds with each one.
2 Add the grated lemon zest and fold in the flour and remaining almonds. Stir in the lemon juice.
3 Spread the frangipane over the cooled pastry base. Lay the plums, cut side up on the almond filling. Bake for 20-25 minutes until golden.
4 Brush the pizza with the syrup. Sprinkle lemon parmesan on top.

chapter two
menus for six

fish extravaganza

serves 6

devilled whitebait

roast cod and crisp shrimps
with lemon butter sauce and gremolata potatoes

roast figs
with parfait and port syrup

F ish lovers will enjoy this menu featuring two courses of fish – crispy devilled whitebait and succulent cod with shrimps, both providing delightfully contrasting tastes and textures. A luscious pudding – roast figs with creamy parfait and port syrup – completes this feast.

Shopping list

7 lemons
12 figs
2 garlic cloves
bunch flatleaf parsley
3 x 250g bags spinach leaves
900g (2lb) floury potatoes
6 x 175-225g (6-8oz) portions of cod fillet, skin left on
650g (1lb 7oz) whitebait
175g (6oz) brown shrimps
55ml (2fl oz) chicken stock (see page 10)
125ml (4fl oz) double cream or milk
milk for coating
550g (1lb 4oz) unsalted butter
300ml (10fl oz) whipping cream
4 eggs
vegetable oil for deep frying
200g (7oz) plain flour
140g (5oz) caster sugar
115g (4oz) soft, dark brown sugar
115g (4oz) sugar
115g (4oz) finely chopped hazelnuts
1½ tbsp hazelnut oil or melted butter
3 tbsp ginger syrup (from stem ginger)
cayenne pepper
crusty bread
nutmeg
white pepper
icing sugar
150ml (5fl oz) port

Prepare ahead

The day before

Bake the hazelnut tuiles, cool and store in an airtight container

Make the port syrup, cool and cover

Prepare the parfait and freeze

Beat the gremolata butter and keep it in the fridge

On the day

45 minutes before sitting down to eat

Cook the potatoes, mash with the gremolata butter and keep warm

Butter and flour the cod fillets

15 minutes before sitting down to eat

Heat the deep-frying oil, coat the whitebait in flour and fry in batches. Sprinkle with salt and serve hot

Pre-heat the oven for the cod

Between the starter and main course

Fry the cod and put in the oven to roast

Fry the shrimps

Make the lemon butter sauce

Wilt the spinach

Assemble the main course

Leave the oven on for the figs

Between the main course and pudding

Put the figs in the oven to roast

Assemble the tuiles and parfait on plates and drizzle with syrup. Finish the figs under a hot grill, place on top of the tuiles.

devilled whitebait

Whitebait (baby herring or sprats) are available frozen throughout the year, but are in season from February to August. For a fuller flavour buy fresh ones if possible.

you will need

preparation time
20 minutes

cooking time
5 minutes

650g (1lb 7oz) whitebait, defrosted if bought frozen
vegetable oil for deep frying
milk for coating
55g (2oz) plain flour
salt
cayenne pepper

lemon wedges, to serve
crusty brown bread and butter, to serve

1 Put the oil in a deep saucepan or deep-fat fryer and heat to 190°C/ 375°F/gas 5. This guarantees the fish cooks quickly and is crisp.
2 Sort through the whitebait and discard any ones that are bruised or broken. Gently wash the remainder and dry on a clean cloth.
3 Pour the milk into a shallow dish. Put the flour in a plastic bag and season with plenty of salt and cayenne pepper.
4 Put the whitebait, a handful at a time, into the milk; then transfer them to the bag of seasoned flour and toss them gently to ensure a good even coating.
5 Carefully place the floured whitebait into the hot fat in batches of one or two handfuls. Cook each batch for about 1 minute until golden and crisp. Lift from the hot fat with a slotted spoon and drain well on kitchen paper.

to serve
While still hot, sprinkle the whitebait with salt. Serve the fish immediately with the wedges of lemon and slices of crusty brown bread and butter.

roast cod and crisp shrimps
with lemon butter sauce and gremolata potatoes

Pan-fried cod finished in the oven is delicious, especially when the skin is left on to give a crispy topping. Small brown shrimps are ideal for this dish. Frying them in nut-brown butter makes them very crunchy. If small brown shrimps are unavailable, use shelled shrimp or peeled prawns.

you will need
preparation time *30 minutes*
cooking time *25 minutes for the potatoes and spinach; 4-6 minutes for the fish; 10 minutes for the sauce*

for the cod and shrimps
6 x 175-225g (6-8oz) portions of cod fillet, skin left on
3 tbsp plain flour
85g (3oz) unsalted butter, very soft
175g (6oz) brown shrimps
1 lemon
salt and pepper

for the gremolata potatoes
900g (2lb) floury potatoes, peeled and quartered
2 garlic cloves, crushed
juice and finely grated zest of 2 lemons
115g (4oz) unsalted butter, softened
salt and pepper
bunch flatleaf parsley, chopped
125ml (4fl oz) double cream or milk
freshly grated nutmeg

for the lemon butter sauce
225g (8oz) unsalted butter, cut into 1cm (½in) cubes
juice of 1 lemon
55ml (2fl oz) chicken stock (see page 10)
salt and white pepper

for the spinach
3 x 250g bags spinach leaves
knob of butter
salt and pepper

roasting the cod
1 Pre-heat the oven to 200°C/ 400°F/gas 6.
2 Lightly dust the skin side of the cod fillets with flour and spread a little butter on each.
3 Heat an ovenproof frying-pan and add half the remaining butter. Once bubbling, add the cod fillets, skin side down. Fry for 2-3 minutes until the skin becomes golden and is starting to crisp. Turn the fillets over in the pan, leaving them skin side up. Finish in the oven for 4-6 minutes.

4 To cook the shrimps, heat the remaining butter in a frying-pan. When bubbling and beginning to turn brown, add the shrimps.
5 Fry the shrimps for approximately 1 minute until crisp. Add a squeeze of fresh lemon juice and season.

making the gremolata potatoes
1 Boil the potatoes in salted water for about 25 minutes (depending on size) until tender. Drain off the water from the potatoes and replace the lid. Shake the pan to break them up.
2 Meanwhile, mash the garlic, lemon zest and juice into the butter and season. Add the parsley and mix.
3 Mash together the cream or milk and the butter mix, and add a little at a time to the potatoes. Season with salt, pepper and nutmeg.

making the lemon butter sauce
Put the butter in a pan with the stock and lemon juice. Bring to a simmer, whisking all the time. Don't let it boil or it will split. If it is too thick, add more stock – or lemon juice to make it sharper. Season and serve at once.

cooking the spinach
Wash the spinach and put in a pan with just the water that clings to the leaves. Cook for 3-4 minutes, drain, toss in the butter and season.

to serve
Sit a piece of roasted cod on a bed of spinach and spoon over some crispy shrimps and warm lemon butter. Then add the potatoes.

roast figs
with parfait and port syrup

Prepare everything in advance and you can assemble this elegant dinner party dessert at the last minute.

you will need

preparation time 1½ hours, plus at least 12 hours freezing for parfait

cooking time 15 minutes

12 figs, halved
55g (2oz) butter
icing sugar for dusting

for the hazelnut tuiles
2 egg whites
25g (1oz) caster sugar
115g (4oz) plain flour
115g (4oz) finely chopped hazelnuts
1½ tbsp hazelnut oil or melted butter

for the parfait
4 egg yolks
115g (4oz) soft, dark brown sugar
3 tbsp ginger syrup (from stem ginger)
300ml (10fl oz) whipping cream

for the port syrup
150ml (5fl oz) port
115g (4oz) sugar
juice of 1 lemon

making the tuiles
1 Pre-heat the oven to 180°C/ 350°F/gas 4. On baking parchment, draw around the base of a 20cm (8in) sandwich tin. Turn the paper over and line the baking tray.
2 Whisk the egg whites and sugar to a froth; then mix in the other ingredients to form a paste.
3 Spread half this paste thinly over the marked circle. Bake for 8-10 minutes until golden. Leave to cool and firm slightly before marking the disc into 6 equal wedges. Cool on a wire rack before breaking into wedges. Bake a second disc to make 12 wedges in all.

making the parfait
1 Whisk the yolks and sugar in a bowl over a pan of simmering water until doubled in volume. Remove from the heat and continue whisking until cool.
2 Whip the cream to soft peaks. Add the ginger syrup to the egg whip and fold in the whipped cream.
3 Pour the mix into the 20cm (8in) sandwich tin, to 2.5cm (1in) deep. Freeze for at least 12 hours to set.

roasting the figs
1 Pre-heat the oven to 200°C/ 400°F/gas 6.
2 Brush the figs with butter. Place on a baking sheet, cut side down, and roast for 4-5 minutes until soft.
3 Turn the figs over, dust with icing sugar and glaze under a very hot grill.

to serve
Boil all the ingredients for the port syrup with 100ml (3½fl oz) water until sticky, then drizzle in zig-zags across the plates. Cut the parfait into 6 wedges, sandwich each between two wedges of tuile and place in the centre of the plates. Arrange the hot figs on top and dust with icing sugar.

stress-free dinner

serves 6

chicken liver parfait
with grape chutney

pan-fried sea bass
with oriental spring onions

Turkish delight ice-cream
with rich chocolate cream

Effective planning and simple cooking take the strain out of giving a dinner party, ensuring the evening is relaxing for host and guests alike. This menu has been designed so that the starter and dessert can be made well in advance. On the day, you just need to cook the sea bass and make the dressing.

Shopping list

I onion
bunch of spring onions
I red chilli
900g (2lb) potatoes
5 Granny Smith or Golden Delicious apples
Ikg (2lb 4oz) seedless white grapes
I garlic clove
275g (9½oz) chicken livers
6 x 175-225g (6-8oz) sea bass fillets, skin on
dash of chicken stock (see page 10)
150ml (5fl oz) milk
125ml (4fl oz) single cream or milk
I large egg
400ml (14fl oz) double cream
170g (6oz) unsalted butter
500ml (1 pint) good-quality vanilla ice-cream
plain flour
150ml (5fl oz) balsamic vinegar
olive oil or sesame oil
sunflower or vegetable oil for frying
light soy sauce
mirin, rice wine or rice vinegar
40g (1½oz) caster sugar
175g (6oz) demerara sugar
225g (8oz) good-quality plain chocolate
natural essence of rose water
175-225g (6-8oz) Turkish delight
whole nutmeg
mixed spice
ground cinnamon
ground ginger
five-spice powder
brandy

Prepare ahead

The week before

Prepare the grape chutney
Prepare the Turkish delight ice-cream

Two days before

Trim and soak the chicken livers in milk
Prepare the rich chocolate cream

The day before

Prepare the chicken liver parfait
Make the mash

On the day

1½ hours before guests arrive

Prepare the dressing for the fish
Deep-fry the fish skins for use as garnish (optional)
Arrange the chicken liver parfait and grape chutney on plates and cover

Between the starter and main course

Remove the ice-cream from the freezer
Pan-fry the fish
Reheat the dressing and the mash

Between the main course and pudding

Warm the rich chocolate cream

chicken liver parfait
with grape chutney

This is really a pâté, but its incredibly smooth, light texture means it eats more like a creamy, whipped parfait. Garnish with a few crispy salad leaves, and serve with grape chutney and toast or bread.

you will need
preparation time
40 minutes plus 24 hours soaking and 4-5 hours chilling for the parfait; 30 minutes for the chutney
cooking time *1-1½ hours for the parfait; 3-4 hours for the chutney*

for the parfait
275g (9½oz) fresh chicken livers, soaked for 24 hours in milk
1 garlic clove, crushed
pinch of freshly grated nutmeg
salt and pepper
1 large egg
325ml (11fl oz) double cream
1 tbsp brandy
1 tbsp chicken stock (see page 10)

for the chutney
makes about 1kg (2lb 4oz)
5 Granny Smith apples, peeled, cored and chopped
1 onion, finely chopped
150ml (5fl oz) balsamic vinegar
150ml (5fl oz) brandy
1kg (2lb 4oz) seedless white grapes, washed
175g (6oz) demerara sugar
salt
1 tsp mixed spice
1 tsp ground cinnamon
½ tsp ground ginger

making the parfait
1 Pre-heat the oven to 160°C/325°F/gas 3. Butter a 450g (1lb) loaf tin and line with greaseproof paper.
2 Drain the milk from livers. In a food processor, blitz the livers with the garlic, nutmeg and seasoning until smooth.
3 Add the egg and blitz for a further minute. Add the cream, brandy and stock. Blitz for a few seconds and check seasoning. Strain the mixture through a fine sieve.
4 Pour the mixture into the loaf tin and cover the top with foil. Stand in a roasting tin and fill three-quarters full with hot water. Place in the oven. After 1 hour, check every 10 minutes until firm to the touch. Leave to cool, then chill for 4-5 hours.
5 To serve, turn out and slice. Covered in plastic wrap and refrigerated, the parfait keeps for 2-3 days.

making the chutney
1 Simmer the apples, onion, vinegar and brandy together in a pan for 30 minutes. Stir in the grapes, sugar, salt and spices and continue to simmer, uncovered, for 3-4 hours over a low heat, stirring occasionally, until the mixture is thick and pulpy.
2 Cool, then spoon into heat-sterilized jars, seal and store in a cool place.

pan-fried sea bass
with oriental spring onions

The delicately flavoured sea bass is given a special lift by the spring onions, spiced up with fresh chilli and a dressing of mirin and soy sauce, which sinks into a bed of creamy mashed potatoes. If sea bass is unavailable, fresh salmon works just as well. Deep fried, both types of fish skins make great crackling.

Cook's notes

Mirin is a Japanese sweet rice wine, available from most major supermarkets, oriental food shops and some delicatessens. It's worth searching it out, but if you can't find mirin, rice wine or rice vinegar make perfectly acceptable alternatives.

Soy sauce comes in light and dark varieties. The light sauce is milder than the dark and works better with the delicate flavour of fish.

you will need
preparation time *45 minutes – including mashed potatoes*
cooking time *10-15 minutes*

for the dressing
3 tbsp light soy sauce
4 tbsp mirin, rice wine or rice vinegar
pinch of five-spice powder
4 tbsp sesame oil or olive oil
salt and pepper
1 bunch of spring onions, finely shredded
1 red chilli, very finely chopped

for the fish
6 x 175-225g (6-8oz) sea bass fillets, skinned and skins reserved
plain flour for dusting
oil for deep-frying fish skin
knob of unsalted butter
salt and pepper

for the mashed potato
900g (2lb) potatoes
115g (4oz) unsalted butter
125ml (4fl oz) single cream or milk

1 To make the dressing, boil the soy sauce, mirin and a pinch of five-spice powder together. Remove from the heat, mix with the sesame or olive oil and season with salt and pepper. Mix the spring onions with the chilli.
2 Dry the reserved fish skins on a cloth and cut into 2.5-5cm (1-2in) wide strips. Lightly flour and deep-fry until crisp. Drain on kitchen paper, season with salt and set aside.
3 Lightly flour the sea bass on the skinned side and season with salt and pepper. Heat a frying-pan and add the butter. Once the butter is bubbling, cook the bass on the floured side for 2-3 minutes; turn it over and continue to cook for a

further 4 minutes. (Depending on the thickness of the fillets, the fish may take a little longer to cook.)
4 Once the fish is turned over, heat 2-3 tbsp of the dressing in a separate pan and add the spring onions and chilli. Cook on a high heat for 1-2 minutes to ensure even cooking.

making the mashed potato
Follow the instructions on page 46 to make up creamy mashed potato.

to serve
Spoon a neat mound of mashed potatoes at the back of each plate and top with a piece of crispy fish skin. Sit a piece of sea bass at the front of each plate and spoon the spring onion and chilli mix on top. Finish by trickling some of the cold dressing around each piece of fish.

Tip Start with
I tbsp of
rose-water,
and check the taste
before adding more,
to get the depth of
flavour you prefer.

Turkish delight ice-cream
with rich chocolate cream

Round off the meal with an exotic ice-cream – simplicity itself to make, but wonderful to eat. Adding rose-water and diced Turkish delight to bought vanilla ice-cream gives it an eastern flavour and a lovely texture. The warm, rich chocolate sauce provides a delicious finishing touch.

you will need
preparation time *20 minutes*
cooking time *20 minutes*

for the ice-cream
500ml (1 pint) tub good-quality vanilla ice-cream, softened
1-2 tbsp rose-water
175-225g (6-8oz) Turkish delight

for the chocolate cream
225g (8oz) good-quality plain chocolate
150ml (5fl oz) milk
75ml (2½fl oz) double cream
40g (1½oz) caster sugar
25g (1oz) unsalted butter

flavouring the ice-cream
1 Beat the softened ice-cream. Stir in the rose-water and mix well.
2 Cut the Turkish delight into small dice with scissors or a warm knife and fold into the ice-cream.
3 Return the ice-cream to the freezer and allow to re-freeze.

making the chocolate cream
1 Melt the chocolate in a bowl over a pan of hot water. Bring the cream, milk and sugar to the boil together, then stir into the melted chocolate.
2 Add the butter to give the sauce a beautiful gloss. Serve warm in a jug for guests to help themselves.

tastes of the Caribbean

serves 6

jerked chicken wings

grilled swordfish
with sweet-sour relish and
sweet potato roasties

baked tropical fruits
with coconut ice-cream

Inspired by the flavours of the Caribbean, this menu is ideal for the summertime or to put you and your guests in a holiday mood. Spicy chicken wings are followed by succulent swordfish, and for dessert – a selection of tropical fruits baked with a hint of rum.

Shopping list

2 bunches spring onions
6 Jalapeno peppers
900g (2lb) sweet potatoes
3 garlic cloves
fresh oregano and thyme
2 lemons and 2 oranges
1 fresh coconut
6 firm bananas
1 ripe pineapple
2 nectarines
450g (1lb) ripe tomatoes
115g (4oz) carrots
2 celery sticks; 1 large onion
1 green pepper
6 x 225g (8oz) swordfish steaks
900g (2lb) chicken wings
150ml (5fl oz) fresh orange juice
225ml (8fl oz) milk
175ml (6fl oz) double cream
55-85g (2-3oz) unsalted butter
5 eggs
115g (4oz) sweetcorn kernels
2 tbsp ground pimento (Jamaican allspice)
1 tsp ground cinnamon
¼ tsp ground nutmeg
½ tsp crushed dried chillies
1 tbsp mustard seeds
75ml (2½fl oz) tomato purée
100ml (3½fl oz) red wine vinegar
150ml (5fl oz) white wine vinegar
vegetable oil
180ml (6fl oz) soy sauce
75ml (2½fl oz) olive oil
55g (2oz) soft brown sugar
175g (6oz) caster sugar
200ml (7fl oz) coconut milk
4 tbsp rum

Prepare ahead

The day before

Prepare the jerk seasoning, rub over the chicken wings and leave in the fridge to marinate overnight

Make the relish, cool and store in the fridge

Make the coconut ice-cream

On the day

2-3 hours before guests arrive

Mix the marinade ingredients for the swordfish, pour over the fish and leave for at least 1 hour

Peel and shape the sweet potatoes, then parboil and drain

1 hour before guests arrive

Brown the sweet potatoes

Parcel up the fruits ready for baking and keep in the fridge

15 minutes before sitting down to eat

Roast the chicken wings and the sweet potatoes

Between the starter and main course

Grill the swordfish

Between the main course and pudding

Put the fruit parcels in the oven

jerked chicken wings

Jerk seasoning is a carnival of Caribbean flavours – you taste sweet and sour, hot and spicy in every mouthful.

you will need

preparation time
30 minutes plus at least 2 hours marinating in fridge

cooking time
40-45 minutes

900g (2lb) chicken wings
vegetable oil

for the jerk seasoning
2 tbsp ground pimento
1 tsp ground cinnamon
¼ tsp ground nutmeg
2 bunches spring onions, chopped
6 Jalapeno peppers, cut in half lengthways
1 tbsp fresh thyme leaves
100ml (3½fl oz) red wine vinegar
2 tbsp vegetable oil
salt and pepper
2 tbsp soy sauce

marinating the wings

1 Combine all the jerk seasoning ingredients in a large bowl.

2 Put the chicken wings in the bowl and stir to make sure that they are thoroughly coated in the seasoning.

3 Cover and chill in the fridge for at least 2 hours, or overnight if it is more convenient.

roasting the wings

1 Pre-heat the oven to 200°C/400°F/gas 6.

2 Heat a strong roasting tin on the hob with a little vegetable oil. When hot, add the marinated chicken wings and fry until they are well coloured.

3 Transfer to the oven for 10-15 minutes.

to serve

Place the hot chicken wings in a large bowl and let your guests help themselves. Supply finger bowls – small bowls of warm water with a slice of lemon – and paper napkins for cleaning fingers.

grilled swordfish
with sweet-sour relish and sweet potato roasties

Swordfish is a wonderfully meaty fish which is best served slightly undercooked in the centre, like tuna. The colourful sweet-sour relish adds a barbecue note and the banana-shaped sweet potato roasties are clearly influenced by the Caribbean.

you will need
preparation time *30 minutes plus 1-3 hours marinating in the fridge*
cooking time *40-45 minutes*

6 x 225g (8oz) swordfish steaks
900g (2lb) sweet potatoes
vegetable oil for roasting

for the marinade
150ml (5fl oz) soy sauce
150ml (5fl oz) fresh orange juice
75ml (2½fl oz) olive oil
75ml (2½fl oz) tomato purée
3 garlic cloves, crushed
1 tbsp lemon juice
1 tbsp chopped fresh oregano
pepper

for the relish
115g (4oz) carrots, finely diced
2 celery sticks, finely diced
1 large onion, finely chopped
1 green pepper, finely chopped
150ml (5fl oz) white wine vinegar
450g (1lb) ripe tomatoes, skinned, deseeded and chopped

55g (2oz) caster sugar
1 tbsp mustard seeds
½ tsp crushed dried chillies
115g (4oz) sweetcorn kernels (thawed if frozen)
salt and pepper

marinating the fish
1 Whisk together all the marinade ingredients in a bowl.
2 Arrange the swordfish steaks in a single layer in the bottom of a large dish and pour over the marinade. Leave to sit in the fridge for at least 1 hour or up to 3 hours. (Don't marinate the fish for any longer – the acid in the orange and lemon juice will 'cook' the fish).

roasting the sweet potatoes
1 Peel the sweet potatoes and cut them crossways into 5cm (2in) lengths. Cut each into quarters lengthways and shape each piece into a banana curve with a small knife.
2 Parboil the sweet potatoes for 3-4 minutes, then drain.

3 Pre-heat the oven to 200°C/400°F/gas 6.
4 Heat the oil in a roasting tin on top of the stove and fry the sweet potatoes until they have a golden brown tinge.
5 Place the sweet potatoes in the oven for 20-30 minutes until deeply browned and tender.

making the relish
1 Blanch the carrots and celery in boiling water for 30 seconds. Drain and put in a pan with the onion and green pepper.
2 Pour in the white wine vinegar and simmer for 10-15 minutes until reduced by half.
3 Add the tomatoes and the rest of the relish ingredients. Cook for 15 minutes, stirring regularly to prevent sticking, until the tomatoes have broken down and the relish is thick but not too dry. Leave to cool before chilling.

grilling the swordfish
1 Heat a chargrill pan until it is very hot. Drain the marinade from the swordfish steaks and reserve.
2 Keeping the heat high, lay the swordfish steaks on the grill pan and sear for 2-3 minutes.
3 Turn over and sear on the other side for another 2-3 minutes.

to serve
Arrange a swordfish steak on each plate, garnished with a heaped tablespoon of relish. Boil the rest of the marinade until reduced by half and serve in a jug, along with the sweet potato roasties.

baked tropical fruits
with coconut ice-cream

The scents of baked bananas, fresh pineapple, rum and orange are stupendous. Scoops of coconut ice-cream and flaked coconut provide the final exotic touches.

you will need
preparation time *30 minutes*
cooking time *40 minutes plus freezing time*

for the coconut ice-cream
1 fresh coconut
175ml (6fl oz) double cream
225ml (8fl oz) milk
115g (4oz) caster sugar
5 egg yolks
200ml (7fl oz) coconut milk
flakes of fresh coconut for garnish

for the baked tropical fruits
6 firm bananas, peeled
juice of 1 lemon for rubbing over the bananas to stop them browning after peeling
1 ripe pineapple, peeled and thickly sliced, core removed
2 nectarines, each stoned and cut into 12 slices
4 tbsp rum
juice of 2 oranges
grated zest of 1 orange
55-85g (2-3oz) unsalted butter
55g (2oz) soft brown sugar

making the ice-cream
1 Crack the coconut and dig out a quarter of the white flesh. Chop it finely and mix with the cream and milk. Bring to the boil.
2 While the milk mix is heating up, whisk the sugar and egg yolks in a large bowl until pale and frothy.
3 Pour the boiling milk mix over the whisked eggs, stirring all the time to form a custard. Sit the bowl over a pan of simmering water, making sure its base does not touch the water. Stir until the custard has thickened.
4 Blitz the custard in a blender until the coconut is shredded, then cool.
5 Add the coconut milk. If you are using an ice-cream maker, churn the mix until it begins to firm up. Transfer it to a plastic container and put it in the freezer to finish freezing. Alternatively, just pour the cooled coconut custard into a plastic container and put it straight into the freezer. Stir it vigorously from time to time to stop large ice crystals forming.

baking the fruit
1 Pre-heat the oven to 200°C/400°F/gas 6. Cut 6 squares of greaseproof paper or foil large enough to wrap the fruit easily.
2 Mix together the rum, orange juice and zest.
3 Place a slice of pineapple in the middle of each square of foil or paper. Cut each banana diagonally in half across the middle and arrange on top of the pineapple with 4 nectarine slices.
4 Top the fruit with a generous knob of butter, a sprinkling of sugar and a drizzle of the rum mix. Scrunch up the paper or foil to seal the parcel and bake in the pre-heated oven for 15-20 minutes until softened. Serve with scoops of ice-cream and flakes of fresh coconut.

exotic mix

serves 6

stuffed vine leaves

Moroccan chicken
with fattoush and couscous

creamy coconut cake
with coconut and apricot filling

Full of rich, exotic flavours, this menu starts with bite-sized stuffed vine leaves, followed by a satisfying main course of Moroccan chicken served with fattoush and couscous. For dessert, a creamy, moist coconut cake makes a wickedly sweet treat.

Shopping list

24 preserved vine leaves
5 onions
1 celery stick
5-7 tomatoes
1 bag of watercress salad
1 cucumber
4 spring onions
1 clove garlic
large bunch fresh parsley
small bunch fresh mint
3 lemons
225g (8oz) minced lamb
6 chicken pieces or 1 large chicken, jointed
25g (1oz) butter, plus extra for greasing
6 eggs
284ml carton of double cream
plain flour
olive oil
1 litre carton fresh orange juice
1 litre carton tomato juice
1 pitta bread
85g (3oz) long-grain rice
55g (2oz) pine nuts
115g (4oz) blanched almonds
115g (4oz) pitted black and green olives
225g (8oz) canned chick-peas
saffron, ground cinnamon, sumac
packet couscous
225g (8oz) caster sugar
225g (8oz) desiccated coconut
175g (6oz) ready-to-eat dried apricots
vanilla essence
freshly grated coconut (optional)

Prepare ahead

The day before
Make the coconut cake, wrap in greaseproof paper and put in an airtight tin
Make the Moroccan chicken (unless making on the day); refrigerate overnight

On the day
2-3 hours before guests arrive
Soak the vine leaves in warm water

1½ hours before guests arrive
Make the stuffing for the vine leaves and set aside to cool
Assemble the Moroccan chicken (unless made the day before) and start cooking it

45 minutes before guests arrive
Stuff and cook the vine leaves
Make the fattoush, but don't add the pitta bread
Poach the apricots and make the coconut syrup for the cake

30 minutes before guests arrive
Add the onions, chick-peas, olives and almonds to the Moroccan chicken
Whip the cream and assemble the cake

Between the starter and main course
Make the couscous
Briefly toast the pitta, then shred it and add to the fattoush
Reheat the Moroccan chicken (if necessary) and add the lemon juice and chopped parsley

Between the main course and pudding
Decorate the cake with coconut shavings

stuffed vine leaves

Delicious savoury morsels, stuffed vine leaves, or dolmas as they are traditionally known, make an attractive starter. You can easily make them for vegetarians using lentils or minced Quorn.

you will need
preparation time
15 minutes plus soaking time
cooking time 50 minutes

24 preserved vine leaves, drained
4 tbsp olive oil
½ onion, finely chopped
1 celery stick, finely chopped
225g (8oz) minced lamb
1 tomato, chopped
85g (3oz) long-grain rice
55g (2oz) pine nuts
3 tbsp finely chopped parsley
salt and pepper
600ml (1 pint) tomato juice

1 If the vine leaves have been preserved in brine, leave them to soak in warm water for an hour.

2 Heat the olive oil in a large frying-pan, add the onion and celery and cook until soft.

3 Add the lamb, tomato, rice, pine nuts and parsley and fry until the lamb is cooked. Add 450ml (16fl oz) of water and simmer until the rice is cooked. Season with salt and pepper to taste, then set aside to cool.

4 Drain and pat dry the vine leaves with kitchen paper. Spoon 2-3 tsp of the lamb mix into the centre of each leaf, then turn the sides in, roll up and tuck in the ends.

5 Place the stuffed vine leaves in the frying-pan, packing them close together, and pour over the tomato juice. Cover with a lid or a plate and simmer gently for 30-40 minutes until tender. Serve at room temperature.

Moroccan chicken
with fattoush (bread salad) and couscous

Meltingly soft chicken with a saffron sauce studded with olives, almonds and chick-peas is teamed with a watercress and pitta bread salad and easy-to-make couscous. Try to use sumac (a red berry with a sour flavour, often used in Middle Eastern cuisine) available whole or ground in specialist shops.

Recipe option

Moroccan mint tea

2 tbsp green tea
handful of mint leaves
85-115g (3-4oz) sugar cubes

1 Put the tea in a teapot. Boil 1 litre (1 ¾ pints) water. Swill a little over the tea and pour off the water.
2 Add the mint leaves and sugar cubes and the rest of the hot water. Infuse for 6-7 minutes. Serve in small, decorative glasses.

you will need
preparation time 25 minutes
cooking time 2 hours

for the Moroccan chicken
6 chicken pieces or 1 large chicken, jointed
25g (1oz) butter
4 onions, finely chopped
pinch of saffron
1 tsp cinnamon
salt and pepper
225g (8oz) canned chick-peas
115g (4oz) blanched almonds
115g (4oz) mixed olives, pitted
3 tbsp chopped parsley
juice of ½ lemon

for the fattoush (bread salad)
1 pitta bread
1 bag of watercress salad
4-6 tomatoes, roughly chopped
1 cucumber, sliced
4 spring onions, chopped
4 tbsp chopped parsley

4 tbsp chopped mint
juice of ½ lemon
6 tbsp olive oil
large pinch of sumac
1 garlic clove, crushed

for the couscous
1 packet couscous
6-8 tbsp extra virgin olive oil
juice of 1 lemon
2 tbsp chopped fresh parsley

making the Moroccan chicken
1 Melt the butter in a sauté pan and fry the chicken briefly to brown it. Add one of the chopped onions and cover with water. Add the saffron and cinnamon, then season and bring to the boil. Reduce to a simmer and cook for 1 hour until the chicken is tender.
2 Add the chick-peas, the rest of the onions, the almonds and olives. Simmer until the onions are soft, topping up with water as necessary.

Just before serving stir in the parsley and the lemon juice.

tossing the fattoush
1 Put the watercress in a bowl with the chopped tomatoes, cucumber, spring onions, parsley and mint.
2 Make the dressing by combining the lemon juice, olive oil, garlic and sumac in a bowl. Toss the dressing into the salad.
3 Toast the pitta bread under the grill or in a toaster. When cool, tear into thin strips and toss in the salad.

preparing the couscous
1 Pour boiling water on the couscous up to 1cm (½in) above the grains. Cover the bowl.
2 After 5-7 minutes, when the couscous is swollen and has absorbed all the water, fluff up the grains with a fork. Drizzle over the olive oil and lemon juice and add the parsley.

creamy coconut cake

Moist coconut sponge filled with poached apricots and covered in whipped cream makes a very sweet and tempting pudding that goes a long way.

you will need

preparation time *20 minutes*

cooking time *45 minutes*

for the cake

plain flour for dusting

6 eggs, separated

90g (3¼oz) caster sugar

115g (4oz) desiccated coconut

1 tsp vanilla essence

for the filling and topping

150ml (5fl oz) orange juice

175g (6oz) ready-to-eat dried apricots

115g (4oz) desiccated coconut

115g (4oz) caster sugar

1 tsp lemon juice

284ml carton double cream

freshly grated coconut, some toasted, to decorate (optional)

baking the cake

1 Pre-heat the oven to 180°C/350°F/gas 4. Lightly butter a 23cm (9in) cake tin and dust it with flour.

2 Whisk the egg yolks and sugar until the whip is thick and pale. Gently fold in the desiccated coconut and vanilla essence.

3 Whisk the egg whites until stiff and fold into the coconut mixture. Pour into the cake tin and bake for about 45 minutes. Allow to cool and cut into 2 layers.

making the filling

1 Gently heat the orange juice in a small pan until hot, add the apricots, take off the heat and cover. Leave to soak while the cake is cooking.

2 Sprinkle the desiccated coconut with cold water to moisten it and set aside. Put 90ml (3fl oz) water in a pan with the sugar and lemon juice. Simmer for about 5 minutes, then add the moistened coconut and simmer for a few minutes until the coconut is creamy and the sugar dissolves.

3 Remove the apricots from the orange juice and dry them on kitchen paper. Whip the cream until thick.

assembling the cake

1 Spread half the coconut mix on the bottom layer of the cake, arrange the apricots on top and then spread over the rest of the coconut mix.

2 Sandwich the cake together and cover in whipped cream. Decorate with freshly grated coconut, if you wish.

Scandinavian delights

serves 6

smoked salmon
with winter salad and pink salad cream

honey-roast gammon
with baked vegetable purées

prune jelly
almond rice pudding

In this Scandinavian-influenced menu, easily available ingredients are transformed into a delightful dinner. A colourful smoked salmon salad is followed by succulent honey-roast gammon and a sweet prune jelly. Start with a glass of warming mulled wine and make a creamy almond rice pudding to go with the jelly and you have a feast that's ideal for cold-weather entertaining.

Shopping list

1.8kg (4lb) potatoes
1.25kg (2lb 12oz) carrots
3 large swedes
4-6 beetroots; small jar pickled beetroots (for vinegar)
3 small onions
2 sticks celery
fresh sprigs of dill
6 red-skinned dessert apples
1 lemon; 1 orange
140g (5oz) raspberries (fresh or frozen)
smoked salmon for 6
2kg (4½lb) mild-cured gammon joint
850ml (1½ pints) double cream
175g (6oz) butter
2 litres (3½ pints) milk
4 large eggs
300g (10½oz) pudding rice
1kg (2lb 4oz) dried, no-soak, ready-to-eat prunes
2 tbsp clear honey; 100ml (3½fl oz) golden syrup
8 tbsp caster sugar; 6 tbsp demerara sugar
55g (2oz) soft, dark brown sugar; 2-4 tbsp icing sugar
3 tbsp raisins
cornflour; 1-2 tbsp potato flour (or cornflour)
225g (8oz) breadcrumbs
175ml (6fl oz) fresh orange juice
2 large gherkins
nutmeg and cinnamon
English mustard powder; Dijon mustard
34 cloves; 6 cardamom pods; 3 cinnamon sticks
2 bay leaves; 10 peppercorns; paprika
16 blanched almonds; 16 hazelnuts
55g (2oz) ground almonds; 25g (1oz) flaked almonds
white wine vinegar
1.4 litres (2½ pints) red wine (for mulled wine)
600ml (10fl oz) red wine (for soaking prunes)

Prepare ahead

The day before
Make the prune jelly and leave in a cool place overnight to set
Make the swede purée and the carrot and rice purée

On the day

3-4 hours before guests arrive
Start simmering the gammon joint with its aromatic vegetables
Make the mulled wine (if serving) and leave to infuse
Make the winter salad and set aside in a cool place
Peel the potatoes and keep in a pan of cold water
Make the raspberry compôte (if serving)

1-2 hours before guests arrive
Make the rice pudding (if serving) and cook slowly in a double saucepan
Make the pink salad cream, cover and put in the fridge
Glaze the gammon joint and put in the oven to roast

Just before guests arrive
Reheat the mulled wine (if serving); put purées in the oven to heat through
Arrange the smoked salmon and toss the winter salad in a bowl
Put potatoes on to boil

Between the starter and main course
Cook the peas; complete the gravy

Between the main course and pudding
Add cream and almonds to rice pudding (if serving) and sprinkle with cinnamon
Whip the cream for the jelly

smoked salmon
with winter salad and pink salad cream

Afeast for the eye as well as the taste-buds – the red and orange
colours of the winter salad and the smoked salmon are set off
to great effect by the pink salad cream. The colours are hot – the
flavours tangy, refreshing and cool.

1 Dice all the cold cooked
vegetables and apple, onion
and gherkins. Pile into a
bowl, toss, and season.
Set aside in a cool place.
2 Pour the cream into a
bowl and stir in 4-6 tsp
beetroot vinegar. Stir in the
sugar, mustard powder and
seasoning. Add the white
wine vinegar, and whisk until
it just starts to thicken. Pour
into a jug, cover and keep in
the fridge. (The cream
thickens as it stands.)

to serve
Arrange the salmon strips
on a plate and sprinkle with
paprika and dill. Serve with
the salad and salad cream.

You will need
preparation time
1½ hours

for the salmon
smoked salmon strips –
enough for 6 as a starter
paprika, to garnish
fresh sprigs of dill, if
available, or dried dill,
to garnish

for the winter salad
3 large potatoes, peeled
and boiled
4 carrots, peeled and
boiled
4-6 beetroot, boiled and
peeled
2 dessert apples, peeled
1 small onion, peeled
2 large gherkins
salt and pepper

for the pink salad cream
300ml (10fl oz) double
cream
up to 6 tsp vinegar from
pickled beetroot, to make
the cream pink
1-2 tsp caster sugar
1 tsp English mustard
powder
salt and pepper
2-3 tsp white wine vinegar

honey-roast gammon
with swede purée and carrot and rice purée

Winter vegetables baked with cream, spices and butter make tasty dishes to go with the honey-roast gammon. The purées can be made up to a week in advance and kept in the freezer. Defrost them the day before the meal and reheat when needed.

you will need

preparation time 1 hour
cooking time 2½ hours

for the gammon
2kg (4½lb) mild-cure gammon joint
2 carrots, quartered
2 small onions, halved, each half studded with 1 clove
2 sticks celery, sliced into thirds
1 dessert apple, quartered
1 bay leaf; 10 peppercorns
3 dessert apples, cored and quartered
18 stoned prunes, soaked for ½ hour in 300ml (10fl oz) red wine (or water)

for the glaze
55g (2oz) soft, dark brown sugar
175ml (6fl oz) fresh orange juice
2 tbsp clear honey
1-2 tbsp Dijon mustard
about 20 cloves
1 tbsp cornflour, for thickening gravy

for the swede purée
3 large swedes, peeled and chopped
115g (4oz) butter

175g (6oz) very fine, dry breadcrumbs
200ml (7fl oz) double cream
2 large eggs, lightly beaten
100ml (3½fl oz) golden syrup
salt and pepper

for the carrot and rice purée
900g (2lb) carrots, peeled and chopped
125g (4½oz) pudding rice
1 litre (1¾ pints) milk
2 tbsp caster sugar
2 large eggs, lightly beaten
55g (2oz) ground almonds
white pepper; pinch of grated nutmeg
salt and pepper
55g (2oz) very fine, dry breadcrumbs
25g (1oz) butter

cooking the gammon joint
1 Pre-heat the oven to 200°C/400°F/gas 6.
2 Place the gammon in a pan with the carrots, onions, celery, apple, bay leaf and peppercorns. Cover with cold water, bring to boil, cover and simmer for 1½-2 hours. Drain the gammon, discarding vegetables.

3 For the glaze, put all ingredients except the cloves in a bowl, and mix.
4 When the gammon is cool, strip the skin off. Score the fat into a diamond pattern. Stud with cloves and put in a baking dish with the wine from the prunes. Put the apples and prunes around the joint. Add the glaze, and bake for 45 minutes, basting 3-4 times.
5 Put the gammon on a serving dish, with the apples and prunes. Pour the cooking juices into a fat separator to remove fat. Thicken the resulting stock with cornflour and cook for 2-3 minutes. Serve with the purées.

making the swede purée
1 Pre-heat the oven to 150°C/300°F/gas 2. Boil the swedes until tender. Drain and mash until smooth.
2 Add three-quarters of the butter and of the breadcrumbs, and all of the other ingredients, beating them into the swede one at a time. Season.
3 Pour the purée into a buttered ovenproof dish, sprinkle remaining breadcrumbs on top and dot with remaining butter. Bake for 2 hours.

making the carrot and rice purée
1 Follow 'Making the swede purée', step 1, using carrots.
2 Cook the rice in 300ml (10fl oz) salted water. When all the water is absorbed, add the milk and simmer until the rice is soft.
3 Add the rice to the carrots with all other ingredients, except the breadcrumbs and butter, and mix to a purée. Season.
4 Follow 'Making the swede purée', step 3.

rice pudding and compôte

75g (6oz) pudding rice	
25g (1oz) butter	
1 litre (1¾ pints) milk	
1 cinnamon stick, and sprinkling of cinnamon to serve	
3 tbsp caster sugar	
1-2 tbsp double cream (optional)	
up to 25g (1oz) flaked almonds	
140g (5oz) raspberries	
2-3 tbsp icing sugar	

1 Simmer the rice with the butter in 300ml (10fl oz) water.
2 When all water is absorbed, add the milk, cinnamon stick and sugar. Simmer for 5 minutes.
3 Transfer to the top pan of a double saucepan and place over bottom pan of simmering water. Simmer for up to 1 hour, until rice is creamy and quite thick. Add a little boiling milk if it's too thick.
4 To make the compôte, simmer the raspberries with the icing sugar for 2-3 minutes until juices run.
5 Just before serving the rice, stir in cream (optional) and almonds, and sprinkle with cinnamon. Serve with the compôte.

prune jelly

This prune jelly is a sweet, light dessert flavoured with red wine and cinnamon. A creamy almond rice pudding with raspberry compôte makes a warming optional accompaniment.

you will need

preparation time
overnight soaking for prunes
cooking time *10-15 minutes*

500g (1lb 2oz) ready-to-eat prunes	
1 cinnamon stick	
300ml (10fl oz) red wine	
juice of ½ lemon	
2-3 tbsp demerara sugar	
1-2 tbsp potato flour (or cornflour)	
caster sugar, to sprinkle	
double cream, whipped to serve	

1 Soak the prunes overnight, with cinnamon, in enough water to cover.
2 Put the prunes and cinnamon into a saucepan with the red wine and all but 2-3 tbsp of the soaking liquor. Add lemon juice and sugar. Bring to the boil and simmer for 5-8 minutes. Remove the prunes from the liquid and arrange in a serving dish in one layer. Take the saucepan off the heat and discard the cinnamon stick.
3 Put the potato flour or cornflour into a cup, add the reserved liquor and stir until smooth.

4 Pour about half the potato flour liquid into the prune liquor in a thin stream, stirring gently in a figure-of-eight. Add more flour, stirring in a little at a time, until the liquid is thick enough to coat the back of a spoon.
5 Return to the heat and bubble gently for 1-2 minutes. Remove from the heat, allow to cool slightly and pour over the prunes.
6 Sprinkle the top with caster sugar to stop a skin forming. Cool and chill for several hours, or overnight, until set. Serve with the double cream.

traditional roast

serves 6

smoked mackerel pâté
with melba toast

roast pork with cider sauce
with roast potatoes and vegetables

sticky toffee pudding

A classic roast is always a popular option. Here it's pork – with crispy crackling, roast potatoes, vegetables and cider sauce. To start, there's a light, smoked mackerel pâté with melba toast, which can be made with little effort in the minimum of time, and to finish, an all-time favourite – indulgent sticky toffee pudding.

Shopping list

1kg (2lb 4oz) King Edward or Maris Piper potatoes
2 onions
3 red-skinned apples
2 lemons
1.8-2kg (4-4½lb) leg, shoulder or loin of pork, with the bones removed
225g (8oz) smoked mackerel fillet
1 thin-sliced white loaf
280g (10oz) dates
115g (4oz) chopped walnuts (optional)
350g (12oz) soft, light brown sugar
115g (4oz) demerara sugar
4 tsp black treacle
350g (12oz) self-raising flour
vegetable oil
lard (optional)
3-4 tsp coarse-grain mustard
2 tsp bicarbonate of soda
2 tsp vanilla extract
4 eggs
300ml (10fl oz) chicken stock (see page 10)
280g (10oz) unsalted butter
90ml (3fl oz) crème fraîche
1.2 litres (2 pints) double cream
300ml (10fl oz) dry cider
1 litre good-quality vanilla ice-cream (optional)

Prepare ahead

The day before

Make the smoked mackerel pâté and toffee sauce and chill overnight in the fridge
Make the melba toast and keep in an airtight tin

On the day

4 hours before sitting down to eat

Make and bake the sticky toffee pudding

2½ hours before sitting down to eat

Prepare the pork and put in the oven
Peel and boil the potatoes

1½ hours before sitting down to eat

Put the potatoes in the oven to roast
Prepare the other vegetables and measure out the ingredients for the cider sauce

30 minutes before sitting down to eat

Start making the cider sauce; finish it after you take the pork out of the oven to rest so you can use the roasting tin

Just before sitting down to eat

Boil the water for the vegetables
Cover the sticky toffee pudding and warm in the oven; stand the toffee sauce in hot water to warm through

Between the starter and main course

Cook the vegetables; heat the cider sauce

Tip Using the same recipe, you can make an equally tasty smoked fish pâté from smoked eel or good-quality kippers. To sharpen the flavour of any of the pâtés, add 2 tsp horseradish sauce, Dijon mustard or snipped chives to the mixture.

3 Pack the pâté into a large bowl or individual dishes. Cover and put in the fridge to set.

making the melba toast
1 Pre-heat the oven to 180°C/350°/gas 4.
2 Lightly toast 16 slices of thin-sliced white bread on both sides in a toaster or under a hot grill.
3 Remove the crusts and cut each slice horizontally into two very thin slices through the soft untoasted middle. Brush or scrape away any rolled balls of soft white bread on the untoasted side of each slice.
4 Cut each thin slice diagonally in half to make triangles. Arrange without overlapping on a baking tray and put in the oven for 4-5 minutes until curled, crisp and golden. Store in an airtight tin until needed.

to serve
Put a spoonful or two of pâté, or each dish, on a plate with some melba toasts and garnish with lemon quarters.

smoked mackerel pâté
with melba toast

This pâté takes a few minutes to make if you have a hand blender or food processor. It is very smooth and creamy – ideal for spreading on crispy home-made melba toast. Any left-over pâté makes an excellent filling for sandwiches.

you will need
preparation time
10 minutes
cooking time *20 minutes for the melba toast*
chilling time *overnight*

for the pâté
225g (8oz) smoked mackerel fillet, skinned and chopped

6 tbsp crème fraîche
115g (4oz) unsalted butter, softened
juice of ½ lemon
salt and pepper
lemon, to garnish

for the melba toast
1 thin-sliced white loaf

making the pâté
1 In a food processor, or with a hand blender, blitz the smoked mackerel with 2 tbsp crème fraîche until puréed.
2 Add the butter and blitz again. Pour in the lemon juice and remaining crème fraîche. Blend again, then check the seasoning.

roast pork with cider sauce
with roast potatoes and vegetables

Succulent roast pork with crispy crackling is even tastier when served with a creamy apple, cider and mustard sauce and crunchy roast potatoes. Choose your own favourite vegetables to complete the roast feast.

Cook's notes

Leg, shoulder and loin of pork are all good joints for roasting. Leg and shoulder are the most economical but loin is the tenderest and tastiest. To simplify carving, ask the butcher to bone out whichever joint you choose, but to leave the skin on to make sure there's plenty of crackling.

you will need

preparation time *30 minutes*

cooking time *2-2 hours 20 minutes*

for the pork

1.8-2kg (4-4½lb) leg, shoulder or loin of pork, with the bones removed

vegetable oil

salt and pepper

2 onions, halved

1½ tbsp salt, for the crackling

2 tbsp vegetable oil, for the crackling

for the roast potatoes

1kg (2lb 4oz) King Edward or Maris Piper potatoes, peeled and quartered

vegetable oil or lard

salt

for the cider sauce

3 red-skinned apples, cored and quartered

knob of butter

300ml (10fl oz) dry cider

300ml (10fl oz) chicken stock (see page 10)

300ml (10fl oz) double cream

3-4 tsp coarse-grain mustard

salt and pepper

roasting the pork

1 Pre-heat the oven to 190°C/375°F/gas 5.

2 Score lines, about 1cm (½in) apart, through the skin of the joint into the fat below. Pat in the salt and massage the oil over the skin.

3 Arrange the 4 onion halves in a roasting tin and put the pork on top. Roast in the oven for 1 hour 30 minutes. Then check the crackling.

4 By then, the skin should be crispy (leave for a little longer if necessary). Lightly cover the top with foil for the last 30-50 minutes of cooking to prevent it scorching. Don't wrap the joint up tightly or the crackling will go soggy. Remove the crackling before carving – this makes carving easier than if you leave it on.

roasting the potatoes

1 Boil the potatoes for 10 minutes; then drain and shake them in the pan to roughen the surface.

2 After the pork has been roasting for 1 hour, pour off the fat into another roasting tin to cover the base, adding more fat if needed.

Heat, then add the potatoes, coating them in the fat.

3 Sprinkle the potatoes with salt and put in the oven above the pork. Roast for 30 minutes; then turn them over and roast for another 30 minutes until crisp.

making the sauce

1 Cut each apple quarter into 4 slices. Melt the butter in a pan and sauté until golden. Remove from the pan and keep warm.

2 Add half the cider to the pan and boil to reduce by half. Then add the stock and again reduce by half.

3 Stir in the cream and mustard and simmer for 10 minutes to thicken.

4 Remove the pork from the roasting tin. Drain off any fat and pour in the remaining cider. Boil briefly to release any pan residue, then strain and stir into the sauce. Return the apple slices to the sauce and season.

sticky toffee pudding

For the sweet-toothed, this rich sponge and scrumptious sauce is the perfect dessert. Serve with cream or ice-cream for a real treat.

you will need

preparation time *25 minutes*

cooking time *1 hour*

for the pudding

280g (10oz) dates, stoned and chopped

115g (4oz) unsalted butter

350g (12oz) soft, light brown sugar

4 eggs, beaten

2 tsp bicarbonate of soda

350g (12oz) self-raising flour

2 tsp vanilla extract

115g (4 oz) chopped walnuts (optional)

300ml (10fl oz) double cream or 1 litre good-quality vanilla ice-cream, to serve

for the toffee sauce

600ml (1 pint) double cream

115g (4oz) demerara sugar

4 tsp black treacle

making the pudding

1 Pre-heat the oven to 180°C/350°F/gas 4. Butter a 24 x 24 x 5cm (9½ x 9½ x 2in) baking dish or tin.

2 Boil the dates in 425ml (15fl oz) water for about 5 minutes until soft and pasty.

3 Cream the butter and sugar together until pale. Add the eggs and beat well.

4 Add the bicarbonate of soda to the date paste. (This will make the mix fizz.) Quickly beat the dates, flour and vanilla extract into the creamed egg mixture. For an added crunch, add the chopped walnuts.

5 Pour the mixture into the dish or tin and bake for 1 hour until just firm to the touch. Check the colour of the pudding after 45 minutes – if the top looks well browned, lay a sheet of foil on top to stop it singeing before it's cooked through.

making the sauce

Place all the ingredients in a pan over a low heat and stir together until blended; then bring to the boil. Transfer to a jug.

to serve

Pour the sauce over each portion of toffee sponge, together with cream or ice-cream as preferred.

great combinations

serves 6

goat's cheese and spinach tart
with roast tomatoes

stuffed loin of lamb
with glazed carrots and mashed swede and potato

berry fool

This menu uses fresh flavours and simple combinations to create a meal that's as elegant as it is classic. A starter of tangy goat's cheese and spinach tempts the taste-buds in preparation for the juicy loin of lamb to follow. A silky fruit fool ends the meal on a smooth note.

Shopping list

1 small and 1 medium onion
2 shallots
1 garlic clove
1 bag baby spinach leaves
6 vine-ripened tomatoes
675g (1lb 8oz) carrots
675g (1lb 8oz) potatoes
450g (1lb) swede
fresh parsley
fresh mint
225g (8oz) blackberries
225g (8oz) blueberries
1 orange
175g (6oz) fresh soft goat's cheese
425ml (15fl oz) single cream
300ml (10fl oz) whipping cream
250g (9oz) unsalted butter
5 eggs
1.6-1.8kg (3½-4lb) loin of lamb, boned
300ml (10fl oz) ready-made lamb stock
85g (3oz) fresh white breadcrumbs
2-3tbsp cooking oil
1 tbsp redcurrant jelly
whole nutmeg
85g (3oz) caster sugar
55g (2oz) sugar
200g (7oz) plain flour
vanilla essence
almond biscuits (ready-made or home-made (see page 60)

Prepare ahead

The day before

Prepare the stuffing for the lamb. Stuff the lamb, roll and tie it and put it in the fridge
Prepare and cook the goat's cheese and spinach tart, leave to cool, then cover and store in the fridge
Make the fruit purée for the fool, cover and chill in the fridge

On the day

2-3 hours before guests arrive

Complete the fruit fool, spoon into serving dishes and store in the fridge

1½ hours before guests arrive

Put the lamb into the pre-heated oven to roast

15 minutes before guests arrive

If serving the tart warm, heat it through in a moderate oven
Roast the vine-ripened tomatoes, slice the tart and garnish

Just before sitting down to eat

Put the swede and potato on to boil
Remove the lamb from the oven, place on a carving plate, cover with foil and leave to rest

Between the starter and main course

Drain and mash the swede and potato
Cook the glazed carrots
Make the gravy for the lamb

Between the main course and pudding

Decorate the fruit fool with whole berries

goat's cheese and spinach tart

with roast tomatoes

This delicious tart can be served warm or cold. Use very soft, rindless goat's cheese which is sold in logs – it combines well with the spinach and cooks to a gorgeous golden brown.

you will need

preparation time
30 minutes

chilling time
15 minutes for the pastry

cooking time
40-45 minutes

for the pastry
175g (6oz) plain flour
85g (3oz) butter

for the filling
1 small onion, chopped
1 bag baby spinach leaves, washed and torn

25g (1oz) butter
1 garlic clove, crushed
175g (6oz) fresh soft goat's cheese
freshly grated nutmeg
2 eggs
150ml (5fl oz) single cream
salt and pepper

for the roast tomatoes
6 vine-ripened tomatoes
olive oil

making the pastry
1 Follow the instructions on page 8, using the amounts shown here and replacing the egg with 1-2 tbsp water.
2 When chilled for 30 minutes, roll out the pastry and use it to line a buttered, loose-based 23cm (9in) fluted flan tin. Put greaseproof paper on top, weight with baking beans and bake at 200°C/400°F/gas 6 for 15-20 minutes until golden.

making the filling
1 Sauté the onion and garlic in the butter for 3-4 minutes until golden. Add the torn spinach leaves and sauté briefly until just wilted.
2 Mash the cheese with a fork to soften it. Put the spinach mixture in a bowl and beat in the cheese, nutmeg, eggs, cream and seasoning.
3 Spoon the filling on to the pastry and cook at 180°C/350°F/gas 4 for 30 minutes until golden. Leave to cool for at least 15 minutes before serving.

roasting the tomatoes
Put the tomatoes in an ovenproof dish and drizzle with olive oil. Roast in the oven at 200°C/400°C/gas 6 for 10-15 minutes until they are soft but still holding their shape. Serve one with each slice of tart.

stuffed loin of lamb
with glazed carrots and mashed swede and potato

The herby stuffing in this dish is enlivened with a dash of orange, which goes beautifully with the lamb and is complemented by the redcurrant jelly in the gravy. Sweet, tender carrots and a creamy root vegetable mash are ideal accompaniments to this roast.

you will need
preparation time *30 minutes for the lamb; 10 minutes for the vegetables*
cooking time *1 hour 30 minutes for the lamb; 20 minutes for the vegetables*

for the lamb

1.6kg-1.8kg (3½-4lb) loin of lamb, boned
2 shallots, finely chopped
25g (1oz) butter
85g (3oz) fresh white breadcrumbs
1 tbsp chopped parsley
½ tbsp chopped mint
1 tsp grated orange rind
salt and pepper
2 tbsp orange juice
1 egg, beaten
2-3 tbsp cooking oil

for the gravy
1 onion, sliced
1 tsp plain flour
300ml (10fl oz) ready-made lamb stock
1 tbsp redcurrant jelly
1 tsp grated orange rind
salt and pepper

for the mashed swede and potato
675g (1lb 8oz) potatoes, peeled
450g (1lb) swede, peeled
55g (2oz) unsalted butter
125ml (4fl oz) single cream or milk
salt and pepper

for the glazed carrots
675g (1lb 8oz) carrots, peeled, topped and tailed
55g (2oz) butter
55g (2oz) sugar
salt and pepper

roasting the lamb
1 To prepare the stuffing, cook the shallots in the butter until soft but not browned. Stir them into the breadcrumbs and add the parsley, mint and orange rind. Season with salt and pepper. Stir well and bind with the orange juice and the lightly beaten egg.
2 If the meat is tied and rolled, untie it. Lay it flat and spread the stuffing over the inside. Roll up and tie securely with string in several places.

3 Pre-heat the oven to 200°C/400°F/gas 6.
4 Heat the oil in a roasting tin and brown the meat on all sides. Place in the oven and roast for 1¼-1½ hours. When cooked, remove from the oven, keep warm and leave to rest for 10-15 minutes.

making the gravy
1 Drain off most of the fat from the roasting tin. Add the sliced onion to the tin and cook on the hob over a medium heat until just softened and turning brown. Sprinkle in the flour and stir to combine.
2 Add the stock, redcurrant jelly and orange rind, bring to the boil and boil briskly for 2 minutes. Season, remove from the heat and strain.

mashing the swede and potato
1 Cut the potato and swede into 2cm (¾in) dice. Place in a pan, cover with water, bring to the boil and simmer for 15 minutes until tender.
2 Drain, add the butter and cream or milk and mash until smooth. Season.

glazing the carrots
1 Cut the carrots into narrow 5cm (2in) sticks. Boil until just tender and drain.
2 Melt the butter in a pan, add the carrots and sprinkle with the sugar. Cook until the sugar dissolves and the carrots are glossy.

to serve
Carve the meat into 1cm (½in) slices. Lay the slices on a warm dish and pour over a little of the gravy. Serve the vegetables separately.

berry fool

Enjoy the flavours of ripe blackberries and blueberries in this creamy dessert. It's enriched with a fresh home-made custard to make it particularly silky and smooth.

you will need

preparation time *25 minutes*

cooking time *20 minutes plus chilling time*

225g (8oz) blackberries
225g (8oz) blueberries
85g (3oz) caster sugar
150ml (5fl oz) single cream
1 egg
1 egg yolk
½ tsp vanilla essence
300ml (10fl oz) whipping cream

almond biscuits, to serve (ready-made or home-made (see page 60)

1 Rinse the fruit and reserve a few berries for decoration. Put the blackberries in a bowl and sprinkle with 25g (1oz) of the sugar. Leave the fruit to soften for 30 minutes, then purée in a processor. Pass the blackberry purée through a fine sieve to get rid of the pips.

2 Meanwhile, place the blueberries in a saucepan with 25g (1oz) of the sugar and 2 tbsp water. Cover and cook gently for 20 minutes or until the fruit is very tender. Allow to cool slightly then purée and refrigerate.

3 Put the single cream in a pan and bring almost to the boil. Lightly whisk the egg, egg yolk, vanilla essence and remaining sugar in a bowl. Pour the hot cream into the egg mixture, stirring constantly, to form a custard.

4 Place the custard over a saucepan of simmering water and stir until thickened. Remove it from the heat and cover with plastic wrap to prevent a skin forming. Allow to cool then refrigerate.

5 Whisk the whipping cream until it forms peaks. Mix the fruit purées into the chilled custard, then fold in the whipped cream. Spoon the fool into glasses and chill for 2 hours before serving with the reserved berries and almond biscuits.

leisurely lunch

serves 6

potted salmon
with wholemeal toast

pot-roast shoulder of lamb
with pommes Parmentier
and roast carrots

apricot sponge

Perfect for a lazy day, this menu involves minimal fuss. After some simple preparations, the dishes are just left to cook or chill. The potted salmon starter can be made a few days in advance. The main course is pot-roast lamb, cooked slowly in a spiced liquor. It's followed by a fragrant, steamed apricot sponge – a comforting conclusion to a mellow meal.

Shopping list

1 orange
2 lemons
900g (2lb) potatoes
600g (1lb 5oz) carrots
2 shallots
1 garlic clove
fresh parsley and tarragon
salad leaves
3 eggs
600g (1lb 5oz) unsalted butter
450g (1lb) salmon fillet
675g (1½lb) shoulder of lamb, boned and rolled
ground mace
cinnamon stick
cloves
black peppercorns
star anise
wholemeal bread
demerara sugar
125ml (4fl oz) light soy sauce
1 x 425g can halved apricots in syrup
18 dried apricots
apricot jam
icing sugar (optional)
milk (optional)
140g (5oz) caster sugar
200g (7oz) self-raising flour
vegetable oil and olive oil
2 glasses dry sherry
white pepper

Prepare ahead

2 days before

Mix up the marinade and pour over the shoulder of lamb; cover and refrigerate

Make the potted salmon, cover and refrigerate

On the day

3 hours before sitting down to eat

Put the lamb in an ovenproof dish, add the water and pot-roast for 2½-3 hours

Soak the dried apricots

Cook the pommes Parmentier and set aside in a warm place

2 hours before sitting down to eat

Make the sponge mix, assemble the pudding and steam for 1¼-1½ hours

Make the apricot sauce

Take the potted salmon out of the fridge

1 hour before sitting down to eat

Uncover the lamb and put the carrots into the oven to roast with it

Just before sitting down to eat

Put the pommes Parmentier in the oven with the lamb to reheat

Serve the potted salmon with lemon, salad and wholemeal toast

Between the starter and main course

Remove the lamb from juices and keep warm. Reduce juices.

Between the main course and pudding

Unmould the dessert, reheat the apricot sauce and serve with cream

potted salmon
with wholemeal toast

If you make this delicious light starter in advance, make sure that you remove it from the fridge in plenty of time so that the salmon can return to room temperature before serving.

you will need

preparation time
25-30 minutes

chilling time
at least 2 hours

350g (12oz) unsalted butter

450g (1lb) salmon fillet

2 shallots, finely chopped

1 small garlic clove, crushed

½ tsp ground mace

½ tsp salt

white pepper

1 tbsp chopped fresh parsley

1 tbsp chopped fresh tarragon

wholemeal bread

a few salad leaves, to garnish

1 lemon, cut into wedges, to garnish

1 Melt the butter and heat until it foams but don't let it brown. Take it off the heat and leave it until the milky residue sinks to the bottom. Strain just the yellow butter fat through muslin. Discard the residue.

2 Trim and skin the salmon fillet and cut it into 1cm (½in) cubes.

3 Warm the clarified butter to simmering point and add the shallots. Cook for a few minutes until the shallots have softened; then add the garlic, mace, salt and pepper.

4 Carefully spoon the salmon into the butter and return to a low heat. Stir very carefully to avoid breaking up the fish. After 5-6 minutes, when the fish is opaque, remove it from the heat and allow to cool. Add the chopped herbs.

5 Spoon the salmon into individual 7.5cm (3in) moulds, making sure that the shallots and herbs are evenly distributed between them. Top up with the remaining butter. Cool, then chill the moulds until set.

to serve

1 About 2 hours before serving, remove the salmon pots from the fridge.

2 Turn out the moulds on to plates and garnish with salad leaves and lemon. Serve with thick slices of hot wholemeal toast.

pot-roast shoulder of lamb
with pommes Parmentier and roast carrots

Shoulder of lamb is one of the tastiest cuts. For this recipe, it has been trimmed of excess fat, then boned, rolled and tied. Marinating the lamb for 2-3 days with the spicy ingredients helps to deepen the flavour. Roast carrots and pan-fried potatoes are perfect side dishes.

Cook's notes

Beurre manié is a paste used for thickening, made by mashing butter and flour to a smooth but still solid consistency.

it to a simmer, skimming off any fat that rises to the top. As the liquid simmers, whisk in the *beurre manié* until it reaches the required thickness. If the sauce tastes too strong, add water.

you will need
preparation time *15 minutes plus 2-3 days marinating*

cooking time *2½-3 hours*

for the lamb
675g (1½lb) shoulder of lamb, boned and rolled

1 orange, cut into 8 wedges

1 lemon, cut into 8 wedges

1 cinnamon stick

6 cloves

10 black peppercorns

2 star anise

2 tbsp demerara sugar

2 glasses dry sherry

125ml (4fl oz) light soy sauce

2-3 knobs of beurre manié (see 'Cook's notes')

for the pommes Parmentier
900g (2lb) potatoes, peeled and cut into 1cm (½in) dice

3 tbsp vegetable oil

55g (2oz) unsalted butter

salt

chopped fresh parsley

for the carrots
600g (1lb 5oz) carrots, peeled and cut into chunks

25g (1oz) unsalted butter

1-2 tbsp olive oil

salt and pepper

roasting the lamb
1 Combine all the ingredients, except the lamb and *beurre manié*. Put the lamb in a bowl, pour over the spicy mix, cover and marinate in the fridge for 2-3 days, turning the meat occasionally.

2 Pre-heat the oven to 160°C/ 325°F/gas 3. Put the lamb and the marinade in a deep ovenproof dish and pour on 450ml (15fl oz) water. The lamb should be about half-covered. Bring to a simmer, and then cover with a lid.

3 Place the dish in the oven and cook for 2½-3 hours, basting every 20 minutes, until the meat is moist. For the last hour, remove the lid.

4 When cooked, remove the lamb, strain the liquor into a pan and bring

cooking the potatoes
1 Wash and dry the diced potatoes.

2 Heat a frying-pan and add a drop of the oil and a knob of the butter. Add just enough potatoes to cover the bottom of the pan and sauté over a medium heat for 10-12 minutes, turning the potatoes so they develop an even golden colour.

3 Transfer to a roasting tin. Cook all the potatoes in this way. Reheat in a hot oven before serving; then season with salt and sprinkle with parsley.

roasting the carrots
1 Melt the butter in an ovenproof dish, and toss the carrots in it. Drizzle with olive oil and season.

2 Place the dish in the oven above the lamb for the last hour of cooking, turning the carrots in the butter and oil once or twice.

to serve
Carve straight through the shoulder of the lamb. Pour the sauce on top and serve with the vegetables.

apricot sponge

Buy ready-to-eat or no-soak dried apricots, which have some moisture left in them, for this recipe. Use apricots that are orange (not brown) and soak them in syrup to make them extra luscious.

you will need

preparation time
30 minutes plus 1 hour soaking

cooking time 1½ hours

1 x 425g can apricot halves
in syrup

18 dried apricots

115g (4oz) unsalted butter

140g (5oz) caster sugar

2 eggs

1 egg yolk

200g (7oz) self-raising flour

milk (optional)

1 tbsp apricot jam

icing sugar, sifted (optional)

1 Pour the syrup from the canned apricots into a pan. Warm through and add the dried apricots. Leave to soak for a few hours until soft.
2 Beat the butter and sugar together until the mix is almost white and the sugar has dissolved.
3 Beat in 1 egg at a time, making sure that the mix is beaten until fluffy after each addition. When both eggs have been added, beat in the yolk.
4 Add the flour and beat until it is completely incorporated into the mixture. Add a little milk if the mix seems dry.
5 Drain the dried apricots from the syrup and place them in a 900ml (1½ pint) pudding basin which has been buttered and dusted with flour. Reserve the syrup. Spoon the sponge mix on top of the apricots until the basin is three-quarters full. Cover the basin with buttered, pleated foil, folding it over the rim and securing with string.
6 Steam the sponge in a pan of boiling water (the water should come halfway up the basin) or in a steamer, for 1¼-1½ hours. Top up the pan with boiling water during cooking, if necessary. When the sponge is cooked, allow it to cool a little in its basin.

making the sauce

1 In a processor, blend the drained canned apricots to a purée. Warm the purée in a pan with the apricot jam; then add enough of the reserved syrup to give a pouring consistency.
2 If the sauce is sharp, add icing sugar to taste. Push through a sieve.

to serve

Turn the cooked sponge on to a plate and spoon the warm sauce over it.

Celtic fare

serves 6

fried cockle salad
with piquant tomato dressing

beef in stout with dumplings
with horseradish mash and
glazed baby carrots

chocolate coffee cake

This hearty meal with Celtic overtones is full of flavours from the sea and the land – crispy fried cockles, a rich beef casserole with Guinness and a sumptuous chocolate coffee cake enhanced with Irish whiskey. Your guests are sure to want second helpings!

Shopping list

bunch fresh parsley
bunch fresh chives
fresh thyme
2 bay leaves
3 garlic cloves
2 green chillies
225g (8oz) onions
2 medium red onions
2 green peppers
1 lemon
10 tomatoes
mixed salad leaves
900g (2lb) floury potatoes
600g (1lb 5oz) baby carrots
1.3kg (3lb) brisket of beef
350g (12oz) fresh cooked cockles
200ml (7fl oz) full-fat milk
300ml (10fl oz) double cream
225g (8oz) full fat soft cream cheese
400g (14oz) unsalted butter
3 eggs
140g (5oz) caster sugar
85g (3oz) plain flour
225g (8oz) self-raising flour
85g (3oz) shredded suet
horseradish cream
280g (10oz) top-quality plain chocolate
6-8 tbsp strong black coffee
coffee beans, to garnish
55g (2oz) ground almonds
almond essence
olive oil plus vegetable oil for deep-frying
600ml (1 pint) Guinness
2-4 tbsp Irish whiskey

Prepare ahead

1-2 days before

Make the tomato dressing

On the day

In the morning

Make the chocolate cake and leave to cool completely
Make the cheesecake cream and refrigerate

3½ hours before guests arrive

Brown the beef and onions, assemble the casserole and put it in the oven

1 hour before sitting down to eat

Make the parsley dumplings
Cook the carrots and reduce the cooking liquor to a glaze
Make the chocolate icing and ice the cake

Just before sitting down to eat

Add the parsley dumplings to the beef to cook
Put the potatoes on to boil
Heat the oil and deep-fry the cockles
Assemble the starter

Between the starter and main course

Mash the potatoes with the other ingredients for the horseradish mash
Reheat the baby carrots in the glaze

Tip The weight of cockles given here refers to shellfish that have been cooked and removed from their shells. Cooked, de-shelled cockles are available from most fishmongers and supermarkets. Make sure you use fresh cooked cockles, not pickled ones.

2 Stir in the olive oil and lemon juice. Add the tomatoes and stir well to break down the tomato flesh slightly. Season with a good pinch of salt, cover and refrigerate.

frying the cockles
1 Heat the oil to 180°C/ 350°F/gas 4 in a deep-fat fryer or deep saucepan.
2 Dip the cockles in the milk, then roll them lightly through the flour, shaking off any excess.
3 Deep-fry the cockles for 1-2 minutes until golden and crispy. It's best to do this in 2-3 batches. Drain on kitchen paper and sprinkle with salt.

to serve
Mix the salad leaves with a few drops of olive oil and season. Arrange the leaves and hot cockles on each plate and spoon the piquant tomato sauce next to them.

fried cockle salad
with piquant tomato dressing

When deep-fried, tiny cockles become crisp and flavoursome. Cook them in a deep-fat fryer or a deep saucepan but be careful because they tend to pop and spit in the hot oil. Don't fry too many at once.

you will need
preparation time
15 minutes for the tomato dressing; 10 minutes for the cockles
cooking time
5-10 minutes

for the tomato dressing
10 tomatoes, skinned, seeded and diced
2 medium red onions, finely chopped
2 green peppers, deseeded and diced
2 green chillies, deseeded and finely diced
1 garlic clove, chopped

3 tbsp olive oil
juice of 1 lemon
salt

for the cockle salad
vegetable oil for deep-frying
350g (12oz) fresh cooked cockles
3 tbsp milk
3 tbsp self-raising flour
mixed salad leaves
a few drops of olive oil
salt and pepper

making the dressing
1 In a bowl, mix the red onions, peppers, chillies and garlic.

beef in stout with dumplings
with horseradish mash and glazed baby carrots

Economical and full of flavour, brisket of beef is ideal for this dish. Long slow cooking mellows the meat and transforms the slightly bitter Guinness into a rich velvety sauce. Creamy potato absorbs this delicious gravy while baby carrots add a splash of colour.

you will need
preparation time *30 minutes for the beef and dumplings; 10 minutes for the vegetables*

cooking time *3 hours for the beef; 25 minutes for the vegetables*

for the beef
1.3kg (3lb) brisket of beef, cubed
2 tbsp olive oil
225g (8oz) onions, peeled and sliced
1 heaped tbsp plain flour
600ml (1 pint) Guinness
2 sprigs fresh thyme
2 bay leaves
2 garlic cloves, crushed
salt and pepper

for the parsley dumplings
175g (6oz) self-raising flour
85g (3oz) shredded suet
1½ tbsp fresh chopped parsley
salt and pepper

for the horseradish mash
900g (2lb) floury potatoes, peeled and quartered
115g (4oz) unsalted butter
150ml (5fl oz) full-fat milk, warmed
salt and pepper
3 tbsp fresh finely chopped chives and parsley
1 tbsp horseradish cream

for the glazed carrots
600g (1lb 5oz) baby carrots
salt
1 tsp caster sugar
55g (2oz) butter

cooking the beef
1 Pre-heat the oven to 140°C/275°F/gas 1.
2 Heat the olive oil in a large ovenproof casserole dish on the hob and brown the meat in batches.
3 Set the browned meat aside and put the onions in the pan. Cook until softened and lightly browned. Lower the heat and return the meat and any juices to the pan. Stir in the flour.
4 Add the Guinness, thyme, bay leaves, garlic and seasoning. Bring to a simmer, cover with a lid and transfer to the oven. Cook for 3 hours until the meat is tender.

making the dumplings
1 Mix all the ingredients in a bowl.
2 Add 4-5 tbsp cold water and mix to a stiff dough. Shape into 6 large dumplings, place on a floured plate, cover and set aside.
3 When the beef has been cooking for about 2½ hours, place the dumplings in the casserole and continue to cook for 20-25 minutes.

making the horseradish mash
1 Boil the potatoes in salted water for 15-20 minutes until tender, then drain them.
2 Mash the potatoes, adding the butter and milk a little at a time. Season, add the herbs and horseradish, and continue mashing until the potatoes are creamy.

making the glazed carrots
1 Put the carrots in a pan with a pinch of salt. Barely cover them with water and add the sugar and butter. Bring to the boil and simmer for 8-10 minutes until tender.
2 Drain the liquor into another pan and boil to reduce to about 6 tbsp of thick liquid. Add the carrots to the pan and reheat in the glaze. Check the seasoning and adjust if necessary.

to serve
Ladle plenty of beef and gravy and a dumpling on to each plate together with helpings of mashed potato and carrots.

chocolate coffee cake

A lmost too good to be true, this wonderfully rich cake is flavoured with coffee and smoky Irish whiskey. Finished with cheesecake cream, it makes a stunning finale to an impressive meal.

you will need

preparation time *1 hour*

cooking time *25-30 minutes*

for the cake
175g (6oz) plain chocolate

4-6 tbsp strong black coffee

2-4 tbsp Irish whiskey

85g (3oz) caster sugar

115g (4oz) unsalted butter, at room temperature

3 eggs, separated

pinch of salt

55g (2oz) ground almonds

few drops of almond essence

55g (2oz) plain flour

coffee beans, crushed, to garnish

for the icing
115g (4oz) plain chocolate

2 tbsp strong coffee

115g (4oz) butter, cubed

for the cheesecake cream
25g (1oz) caster sugar

225g (8oz) full fat soft cream cheese

300ml (10fl oz) double cream, lightly whipped

making the cake

1 Pre-heat the oven to 180°C/ 350°F/gas 4. Butter a 20cm (8in) round cake tin. Dust with flour.

2 Melt the chocolate with the coffee and whiskey in a bowl over a pan of simmering water. Cool to room temperature.

3 Reserve 1 tbsp sugar, and cream the remainder with the butter until fluffy. Beat in the egg yolks.

4 Whisk the egg whites and salt to soft peak stage. Sprinkle on the reserved sugar and continue beating until stiff peaks form.

5 Blend the chocolate into the butter and sugar. Stir in the ground almonds and essence. Fold in 2 tbsp egg white and 2 tbsp sifted flour. Continue folding and sifting alternately until the mix is well blended.

6 Turn the mix into the prepared tin. Bake in the middle of the oven for 25-30 minutes until a skewer pushed into the middle comes out clean. Allow to cool before icing.

making the icing

1 Melt the chocolate with the coffee in a bowl over simmering water. Remove from the heat and beat in the butter a little at a time.

2 Stand the bowl over cold water and beat until the chocolate mix is cool and thick. If it begins to separate, refrigerate for 10 minutes; then beat vigorously with a whisk.

making the cream

1 Beat the sugar into the cream cheese until the sugar has dissolved and the mixture is smooth.

2 Fold in the cream, cover and chill.

finishing the cake

Spread the icing over the cooled cake. Serve in slices, topped with a swirl of cheesecake cream and a few crushed coffee beans.

smart dinner party

serves 6

saffron haddock soup

roast peppered beef fillet
with stilton and red onion salad

cranberry walnut tarts
with whipped vanilla cream

Entertain in style with a spicy saffron haddock soup – an excellent wake-up call for the taste buds – followed by peppered fillet of beef with a tangy stilton and red onion salad. Warmed cranberry walnut tarts with whipped cream provide an elegant finale.

Shopping list

1 leek
1 potato
3 red onions
2 small garlic cloves
350g (12oz) mixed salad leaves
small bunch of coriander
1 lemon
1 orange
350g (12oz) fresh cranberries
675g (1½lb) beef fillet
350g (12oz) natural smoked haddock fillet
350ml (12fl oz) chicken stock (see page 10)
250ml (8fl oz) milk
125ml (4fl oz) single cream
568ml carton whipping cream
70g (2½oz) butter
115g (4oz) stilton cheese
3 eggs
225g (8oz) sweet shortcrust pastry (see page 8, 'variations')
175g (6oz) caster sugar
55g (2oz) soft light brown sugar
55g (2oz) soft dark brown sugar
2-3 tbsp icing sugar plus extra to decorate
175g (6oz) golden syrup
115g (4oz) walnuts
1½ tsp vanilla extract
1 tbsp medium curry powder
saffron strands
1-2 tbsp cranberry jelly
2 tbsp crushed black peppercorns
2 tsp Dijon mustard
2 tbsp red wine vinegar; 2 tbsp balsamic vinegar
4 tbsp walnut oil; 7 tbsp groundnut oil
3-4 tbsp olive oil
1 French stick and 6 bread rolls
3 tbsp port

Prepare ahead

On the day

2-3 hours before sitting down to eat

Roll the beef in the crushed black peppercorns

Make and bake the tart cases; make the filling for the tarts and make the cranberry compôte

1 hour before sitting down to eat

Marinate the red onions for the salad

Make the soup

30 minutes before sitting down to eat

Pan-fry the beef and transfer to the oven to roast; when cooked, set aside in a warm place to rest, covered with foil

Assemble and bake the tarts

Make the dressing for the salad and set aside

Just before sitting down to eat

Reheat the soup

Warm the bread rolls to serve with the soup

Between the starter and main course

Toast the French bread slices and assemble the salad

Slice the beef and toss the salad

Between the main course and pudding

Whip the cream with the vanilla extract to serve with the warm tarts

Tip The wonderful marriage of smoked haddock, curry and rice in kedgeree was the inspiration for this soup. The flavours of the haddock and curry work so well together; the saffron adds extra flavour and a strong colour. To complete the kedgeree theme, you could add a little cooked rice to the finished soup.

simmer. Then put it in the oven for 5-6 minutes.
2 Melt the remaining butter in a saucepan, add the leek, potatoes and garlic, and cook for 2-3 minutes being careful not to let the vegetables colour.
3 Add the curry powder and saffron and cook for a further 2-3 minutes .
4 Remove the cooked fish from its dish and leave to cool. Strain the cooking liquor over the vegetables and simmer until tender, for 15-20 minutes.
5 Liquidize the vegetables and cooking liquor until smooth, then pass through a sieve. Add the cream and the lemon juice and season to taste.
6 Flake the haddock, add most of it to the soup and heat through.

to serve
Garnish with chopped coriander leaves, the rest of the haddock and a few strands of saffron. Serve with warm bread rolls.

saffron haddock soup

This soup's complex flavours blend together extremely well, making it a sophisticated starter. Serve with plenty of warm, crusty bread rolls.

you will need
preparation time
30 minutes
cooking time *40 minutes*

large pinch of saffron strands plus extra to garnish
350g (12oz) natural smoked haddock fillet
350ml (12fl oz) chicken stock (see page 10)

250ml (8fl oz) milk
25g (1oz) butter
1 leek, cut into 1cm (½in) dice
1 potato, peeled and cut into 1cm (½in) dice
2 small garlic cloves, crushed
1 tbsp medium curry powder
125ml (4fl oz) single cream
squeeze of lemon juice

salt and pepper
coarsely chopped coriander, to garnish
crusty bread rolls, to serve

1 Pre-heat the oven to 180°C/350°F/gas 4. Put the smoked haddock in a flameproof, ovenproof dish. Pour the stock and milk over it, add half the butter and bring to a

roast peppered beef fillet
with stilton and red onion salad

Beef and stilton make a robust – and very British – combination. It's so good you'll want to make it time and again. Give the beef depth of flavour by rolling it in crushed black peppercorns several hours before you start to cook.

Cook's notes

To save time if you're in a hurry, instead of making a separate dressing for the salad, simply add a good slug of port and 2 tsp Dijon mustard to the red onion marinade, mix together thoroughly, and toss with the salad. If you are a great stilton fan, try adding some extra crumbled cheese.

you will need

preparation time *30 minutes, plus 1-2 hours marinating*

cooking time *25 minutes, plus resting*

for the beef

675g (1½lb) beef fillet
2 tbsp crushed black peppercorns
1 tbsp groundnut oil or knob of butter

for the dressing

3 tbsp port
2 tsp Dijon mustard
2 tbsp red wine vinegar
4 tbsp walnut oil
4 tbsp groundnut oil
salt and pepper

for the salad

3 red onions
3-4 tbsp olive oil
2 tbsp groundnut oil
2 tbsp balsamic vinegar
1 tbsp lemon juice
350g (12oz) mixed salad leaves
115g (4oz) stilton cheese, crumbled
salt and pepper
10 thin slices of French bread, halved

marinating the onions for the salad

1 Cut the onions into 6-8 wedges, leaving the base intact. Drop carefully into boiling water and cook for 2 minutes.
2 To make the marinade, warm the groundnut oil, 2 tbsp olive oil, balsamic vinegar and lemon juice in a small pan. Drain the onions and place in a non-metallic bowl. Pour on the marinade and season to taste; set aside for 1-2 hours.

roasting the beef

1 Pre-heat the oven to 220°C/ 425°F/gas 7. Roll the beef in the crushed peppercorns.
2 Heat a roasting tin over a high heat on the hob and add the oil or a knob of butter. Fry the beef until deeply coloured all over. Transfer to the oven and roast for 10-12 minutes for medium-rare meat. For medium to well done, roast for up to 20 minutes.
3 Remove from the oven, cover with foil and leave to rest for at least 10 minutes before slicing and serving. Leave the oven on for the bread.

mixing the dressing

1 Boil and reduce the port by half and allow to cool. Mix the mustard with the red wine vinegar.
2 Whisk together the oils and slowly pour into the mustard and vinegar mixture, whisking continuously. Then whisk in the reduced port and season with salt and pepper.

finishing the salad

1 Drizzle the bread with the rest of the oil and toast until crisp. Set aside.
2 Drain the onions and mix with the salad leaves, stilton and a little of the dressing.

to serve

Carve the beef into thin slices and fan 2 or 3 slices on each plate. Add a portion of the salad, trickling some more dressing over it and around the edge of the plate. Place the hot toasts on top of the salad.

cranberry walnut tarts
with whipped vanilla cream

In these little tarts, the sticky texture and nutty flavour – which is rather like a pecan pie – offsets the sharp cranberries beautifully. The tarts are best eaten just warm.

you will need

preparation time *30 minutes*

cooking time *50 minutes*

for the tarts

225g (8oz) sweet shortcrust pastry (see page 8, 'variations')
40g (1½oz) butter
115g (4oz) caster sugar
55g (2oz) soft light brown sugar
55g (2oz) soft dark brown sugar
175g (6oz) golden syrup
1 tsp vanilla extract
2 eggs and 1 egg yolk
115g (4oz) walnuts, roughly chopped
115g (4oz) fresh cranberries
icing sugar to decorate, sifted

for the cranberry compôte

225g (8oz) fresh cranberries
juice of 1 orange
55g (2oz) caster sugar
1-2 tbsp cranberry jelly

for the vanilla cream

568ml carton whipping cream
2 tbsp icing sugar
½ tsp vanilla extract

Cook's notes

To make 1 large tart instead of 6 small ones, use an 18-20cm (7-8in) loose-bottomed flan tin and bake for 40-45 minutes instead of 20 minutes.

preparing the tarts

1 Pre-heat the oven to 200°C/400°F/gas 6. Line 6 small tartlet tins, 9cm (3½in) in diameter, with the sweet pastry. Lay greaseproof paper on top and weight with baking beans. Bake for 20 minutes. Turn the oven down to 160°C/315°F/gas 3.

2 Melt the butter in a saucepan until light brown. Remove from the heat, add all the different sugars and golden syrup, and mix thoroughly.

3 Add the vanilla extract, salt, whole eggs and egg yolk and mix together well. Allow to cool before spooning into the tart cases.

4 Mix the walnuts and cranberries together, spoon over the filling and bake for 20 minutes. Leave the tarts to rest before removing from their tins.

making the cranberry compôte

1 Put the cranberries, orange juice and sugar in a pan. Bring to a simmer and remove the cranberries with a slotted spoon.

2 Add the cranberry jelly and simmer for 5-10 minutes until syrupy.

3 Cool and then return the cranberries to the pan.

to serve

Whip the cream with the icing sugar and vanilla to form soft peaks. Dust the plates with icing sugar, place a warm tart in the centre and pour pools of warm compôte around each one. Serve with the whipped vanilla cream.

super veggie supper

serves 6

almond and celery soup

roast mushroom and leek shepherd's pie
with carrots and petit pois

chocolate terrine
with coffee custard sauce

Here's a menu that will be appreciated by all food lovers, not just vegetarians. Subtle almond and celery soup is followed by an intensely flavoured shepherd's pie packed with savoury roasted mushrooms and sweet leeks. A wickedly rich chocolate terrine ends the meal.

Shopping list

900g (2lb) flat mushrooms
3-4 leeks
450g (1lb) celery
2 onions
1kg (2lb 4oz) floury potatoes
450g (1lb) baby carrots
1 lemon
fresh parsley, tarragon and basil
few sprigs of fresh flatleaf parsley
400ml (14fl oz) single cream
700ml (1¼ pints) double cream
700ml (1¼pints) milk
425g (15oz) unsalted butter
85g (3oz) gorgonzola
17 eggs
450g (1lb) frozen petit pois
115g (4oz) ground almonds
500g (1lb 2oz) caster sugar
1 tsp sugar
450g (1lb) dark chocolate
200g (7oz) cocoa
2 tsp fresh ground coffee
flaked almonds
freshly grated nutmeg
celery salt
olive oil
500ml (18fl oz) ready-made vegetable stock
150ml (5fl oz) dry white wine

Prepare ahead

The day before

Make the chocolate terrine, cover with chocolate coating and refrigerate

On the day

2-3 hours before guests arrive

Make the soup up to the end of step 4 and set aside
Cook the coffee custard sauce, cool and strain

1 hour before guests arrive

Prepare the mashed potato for the shepherd's pie
Roast the mushrooms, cook the leeks and assemble the shepherd's pie; set aside in a warm place
Start cooking the carrots

10 minutes before sitting down to eat

Add the cream to the soup, return to a gentle simmer. Sprinkle with flaked almonds and a few small celery leaves just before serving

Between the starter and main course

Brush the top of the shepherd's pie with melted butter, scatter with the gorgonzola and place in the pre-heated oven for 10 minutes; finish under the grill if desired
Finish cooking the carrots
Cook the petit pois

Between the main course and pudding

Remove the terrine from the fridge, cut into thin slices with a hot knife and serve in a pool of coffee custard sauce

almond and celery soup

This delicately flavoured soup makes an excellent first course for a dinner party. Make sure you use a very good quality vegetable stock to maintain the subtlety of the flavour.

you will need
preparation time
15 minutes
cooking time
45-50 minutes

450g (1lb) celery, roughly diced, reserving a few leaves to garnish

115g (4oz) ground almonds
25g (1oz) butter
½ small onion, roughly chopped
1 small potato, peeled and roughly diced
150ml (5fl oz) dry white wine

500ml (18fl oz) ready-made vegetable stock
250ml (8fl oz) milk
celery salt
pepper
250ml (8fl oz) single cream
flaked almonds, lightly toasted

1 Melt the butter in a large saucepan. Add the vegetables and cook on a low heat, turning them in the butter until all are coated. Sweat with a lid on for 10-15 minutes until they begin to soften.
2 Add the white wine and increase the heat, leaving the lid off to allow the wine to evaporate and reduce.
3 When nearly all the liquid has evaporated, add the ground almonds, stock and milk. Season with the celery salt and pepper, bring to the simmer and cook for 20 minutes. Check that all the vegetables are tender.
4 Remove from the heat and liquidize until smooth. For a smoother consistency, with no grainy texture from the almonds or celery strings, strain through a fine sieve, pushing it all through with a ladle.
5 Add the single cream and return to a gentle simmer. Check the seasoning.

to serve
Sprinkle with flaked almonds and celery leaves.

roast mushroom and leek shepherd's pie
with carrots and petit pois

Shepherd's pie is a classic British dish and this version is absolutely delicious. The flat mushrooms give it a strong flavour and a chewy, almost meaty texture. The dish is assembled in layers, like a lasagne, with cheesy mashed potato on top.

you will need

preparation time *30-40 minutes*

cooking time *10 minutes for the pie; 20 minutes for the carrots; 10 minutes for the petit pois*

for the shepherd's pie

900g (2lb) flat mushrooms, wiped, and stalks removed

3-4 leeks, finely sliced

900g (2lb) large floury potatoes, peeled and quartered

115g (4oz) unsalted butter

125ml (4fl oz) single cream or milk

salt, pepper and freshly grated nutmeg

juice of ½ lemon

1 tsp each chopped fresh parsley, tarragon and basil

olive oil

1 onion, sliced

85g (3oz) gorgonzola, cut into cubes

for the carrots and petit pois

450g (1lb) baby carrots, peeled

1 tsp sugar

25g (1oz) butter plus extra knob

juice of ½ lemon

salt and pepper

450g (1lb) frozen petit pois

few sprigs of fresh flatleaf parsley, torn

making the pie

1 Pre-heat oven to 220°C/425°F/gas 7.

2 Boil the potatoes in salted water for 20-25 minutes until cooked. Drain, and with the lid on the pan, shake vigorously.

3 Add the butter to the potatoes (reserving a knob for later) and mash, adding the milk or cream a little at a time. Season with salt, pepper and freshly grated nutmeg according to taste; stir in the lemon juice and herbs.

4 Heat 1-2 tbsp olive oil in a frying-pan. Season the mushrooms and fry on a high heat, colouring them well. After a minute, turn them and brown the other sides, adding more oil as necessary.

5 Put the mushrooms on an oiled roasting tray and roast for 5-6 minutes. Once cooked, remove and set aside.

6 Heat 1 tbsp of olive oil with half the reserved butter in a frying-pan and add the sliced onion. Cook over a medium heat until softened and lightly coloured. Increase the heat, add the leeks and season. Stir for 3-4 minutes until tender.

7 Cut the mushrooms into slices and fill a buttered ovenproof dish with a layer of mushrooms and a layer of onions and leeks until they are all used up.

8 Spread the potato on top. Melt the remaining butter and brush on to the potato. Dot with the cubes of gorgonzola and place in the hot oven for 10 minutes.

cooking carrots and petit pois

1 Put the carrots in a pan and just cover with water. Add a pinch of salt, the sugar and half the butter, and cover with buttered greaseproof paper. Bring to a simmer and cook until the carrots are just tender. Remove from the pan with a slotted spoon and set aside.

2 Bring the cooking liquor to the boil and reduce by three-quarters until syrupy. Add the lemon juice, increase the heat and simmer for a minute.

3 Reheat the carrots in the sauce, season and add the remaining butter.

4 Cook the petit pois in a pan of boiling water for 3-5 minutes. Drain, toss in butter and season.

5 Tip the petit pois and carrots into a serving dish and sprinkle with parsley.

chocolate terrine
with coffee custard sauce

A rich chocolate terrine makes a magnificent finale to this meal. It freezes beautifully so you can make it in advance.

you will need

preparation time
2 hours, plus 3 hours chilling

cooking time *30 minutes*

for the sponge
225g (8oz) caster sugar
5 eggs, separated
115g (4oz) cocoa

for the mousse
175g (6oz) dark chocolate
175g (6oz) unsalted butter
85g (3oz) cocoa
300ml (10fl oz) double cream
4 eggs, separated
175g (6oz) caster sugar

for the chocolate coating
125ml (4fl oz) milk
70ml (2½fl oz) double cream
280g (10oz) dark chocolate, chopped
70g (2½oz) butter, chopped

for the coffee custard sauce
8 egg yolks
85g (3oz) caster sugar
300ml (10fl oz) milk
300ml (10fl oz) double cream
2 tsp fresh ground coffee

making the sponge

1 Pre-heat the oven to 160°C/325°F/gas 3. Butter and line a 40 x 30cm (16 x 12in) baking tray with baking parchment. Line a terrine mould 29 x 9cm (12 x 3½in) with plastic wrap.
2 Mix half the sugar with the egg yolks and whisk until pale and fluffy.
3 Whisk the egg whites until they form soft peaks, add the remaining sugar and continue to whisk until stiff.
4 Fold the cocoa into the egg-yolk mix. Whisk in a quarter of the meringue; then fold in the rest.
5 Spread the mix in the baking tray. Bake for 20-30 minutes. Leave to cool.

making the mousse

1 Melt the chocolate and butter in a bowl over a pan of warm water until blended and thick. Add cocoa and beat until smooth and cool.
2 Whip the cream until it forms soft peaks and then chill.
3 Whisk the egg yolks with half the sugar until pale and fluffy. Fold into the chocolate mix.
4 Whisk the egg whites with the remaining sugar to meringue stage; then fold into the chocolate mix. Next fold in the whipped cream.
5 Cut the cold sponge into four pieces to fit the base, top and sides of the terrine. Line the base and sides, saving one piece for the top.
6 Pour the chocolate mousse into the mould, and top with the remaining piece of sponge. Chill for 2-3 hours or freeze until firm.

making the chocolate coating

Put the chocolate and butter in a bowl. Bring the milk and cream to the boil and pour into the bowl. Stir until the mixture has blended. Cool to room temperature – this thickens the mixture.

finishing the terrine

When firm, turn the chilled terrine out on to a board. Spoon on the chocolate coating and spread it evenly over the sides and top. Keep chilled or frozen. When the coating has set, cover with plastic wrap.

making the coffee custard

1 Beat the yolks and sugar until fluffy.
2 Put the milk and cream in a pan, add the coffee and bring to the boil. Remove from the heat and strain.
3 Sit the bowl of eggs and sugar over a pan of barely simmering water and whisk in the coffee-cream mix. Stir until the mixture thickens. Cool and strain through a fine sieve.

supper on a shoestring

serves 6

lentil soup
with roast tomatoes and onions

spaghetti and beetroot
with goat's cheese and deep-fried
onion rings

apple and cinnamon sponge

You don't have to compromise on flavour or presentation if you're on a tight budget. Lentil soup with roasted tomatoes and onions looks wonderful and is full of flavour, as is spaghetti paired with beetroot and goat's cheese. For pudding, apple and cinnamon sponge tastes great, especially with custard.

Shopping list

450g (1lb) tomatoes
4 cherry tomatoes
3 large onions
3 medium onions
4 garlic cloves
225g (8oz) beetroot
bag of salad leaves
2-3 large dessert apples
1 lemon
small bunch of lemon thyme
175g (6oz) fresh soft goat's cheese
225g (8oz) butter
2 eggs
568ml tub of fresh custard
milk
flour
crusty bread
1½ litres (2¾ pints) chicken stock (see page 10) or ready-made vegetable stock
175g (6oz) green lentils
1 packet of spaghetti
90g (3¼oz) demerara sugar
115g (4oz) caster sugar
150g (5½oz) self-raising flour
golden syrup
ground cinnamon
bay leaf
Dijon mustard
white wine vinegar
olive oil
1 small bottle vegetable oil for frying

Prepare ahead

The day before
Make the apple and cinnamon sponge (unless making on the day) and put it in the fridge overnight
Roast the onions and tomatoes, allow to cool, cover and put in the fridge

On the day
2-3 hours before guests arrive
Make the soup and set aside to be reheated later

1½ hours before guests arrive
Cook the beetroot; allow it to cool, grate, cover and set aside
If you're cooking the pudding on the day, stew the apples and make the syrup

30 minutes before guests arrive
Soak the onions in milk
Make the sponge for the pudding and put it in the oven
Make the salad and dressing, but don't toss together yet

Just before sitting down to eat
Reheat the soup
Check the sponge; remove from oven when done (or put in the oven on low to reheat)
Dress the salad

Between the starter and main course
Fry the garlic and pasta, add the stock and beetroot
Put the oil on to heat and deep-fry onions

Between the main course and pudding
Turn the sponge out of its tin and heat the custard

lentil soup
with roast tomatoes and onions

Roasting the onions and tomatoes gives this lentil soup a wonderfully rich, satisfying flavour while the lemon thyme adds a citrus edge. Serve it with rustic-style crusty bread and unsalted butter.

you will need
preparation time
15 minutes

cooking time
1 hour to roast the vegetables; 20-30 minutes for the soup

450g (1lb) tomatoes, halved
4 cherry tomatoes
3 large onions, peeled and quartered
small bunch of lemon thyme
olive oil
2 large garlic cloves, crushed

175g (6oz) green lentils
1 bay leaf
850ml (1½ pints) chicken stock (see page 10) or ready-made vegetable stock
salt
crusty bread, to serve

1 Pre-heat the oven to 160°C/325°F/gas 3.
2 Put the onions, large tomatoes and 2 sprigs of lemon thyme in a large roasting tin. Drizzle generously with olive oil and sprinkle with a good pinch of salt.
3 Place in the oven and cook for about 1 hour until soft and browned but not burned. When the tomatoes and onions are nearly cooked, toss in the cherry tomatoes.
4 To start making the rest of the soup, heat the oil in a large saucepan and add the crushed garlic cloves. Fry for 1-2 minutes, taking care not to let them burn.
5 Add the green lentils and fry for 1 minute. Add the stock, bay leaf and 2 or 3 sprigs of lemon thyme. Cook for 20-30 minutes until the lentils are soft.
6 Once the lentils are cooked, add the roasted onion and tomatoes to the saucepan and stir gently.
7 Bring the soup to the boil and simmer for 5 minutes.

to serve
Add a drizzle of olive oil and a sprig of lemon thyme to each bowl of soup and serve with crusty bread.

spaghetti and beetroot
with goat's cheese and deep-fried onion rings

Spaghetti and beetroot is an unusual dish that's very simple and economical to make and looks very colourful and dramatic. The crispness of the deep-fried onion rings works well with the spaghetti and beetroot, and the light crumbling of goat's cheese on top adds a good contrast.

you will need
preparation time 15 minutes
cooking time 15 minutes for the beetroot; 8-10 minutes for the spaghetti

for the spaghetti and beetroot
225g (8oz) fresh raw beetroot or 4 cooked beetroot (not in vinegar)
2 tbsp olive oil
1 onion, chopped
2 garlic cloves, crushed
1 packet of spaghetti
600ml (1 pint) chicken stock (see page 10) or ready-made vegetable stock
175g (6oz) soft goat's cheese

for the deep-fried onion rings
2 onions, peeled and cut into rings
milk and seasoned flour for dipping
small bottle of vegetable oil

for the salad (optional)
assortment of salad leaves – lettuce, watercress and baby spinach
4 tbsp olive oil
1 tbsp white wine vinegar
1 tbsp lemon juice
1 dsp Dijon mustard
salt and pepper

cooking the spaghetti and beetroot
1 Bring a pan of water to the boil and add the un-peeled beetroot. Boil for about 10-15 minutes until al dente, drain and cool.
2 Slip off the skins and grate the beetroot on a coarse cheese grater. (Wear rubber gloves to prevent the beetroot from colouring your hands.)
3 Heat the olive oil in a pan. Add the onion and garlic and fry until soft.
4 Break the spaghetti into 7.5cm (3in) lengths and add to the pan. Fry, stirring often, until golden and toasted.
5 Stir in two-thirds of the stock, bring to the boil and mix in the grated beetroot.
6 Cook for 10 minutes until the spaghetti is soft and the remaining liquid is quite creamy. Top up with a little more stock if it boils dry before the pasta is cooked.
7 When cooked, crumble half the goat's cheese into the mix and stir it in lightly.

frying the onion rings
1 Soak the onion rings in milk for 30 minutes.
2 Put the vegetable oil on to heat or turn on the deep-fat fryer.
3 Drain the onion rings and dust them in seasoned flour.
4 To test if the oil is hot enough for frying, toss in a cube of bread – it should start to sizzle immediately.
5 Plunge the onions into the hot oil for about 5 minutes until they start turning brown. Lift them out of the oil (leaving the oil on a low heat). Shake off any surplus oil and let them stand for 2-3 minutes. Then plunge the rings back into the oil and fry until golden and crisp.
6 Remove from the pan with a slotted spoon and allow to drain and cool a little on kitchen paper.

making the salad (optional)
1 Wash and dry the leaves.
2 Whisk together the oil, mustard, vinegar, lemon juice and seasoning.
3 Put the salad leaves into a large bowl and drizzle over the dressing, whisking all the while as you pour. Toss the salad lightly.

to serve
Pile a serving of pasta on to each plate, sprinkle with crumbled goat's cheese and put some deep-fried onion rings on the side of the plate. Serve the salad separately.

apple and cinnamon sponge

Caramelized apples baked under a light cinnamon sponge make a thrifty and satisfying dessert. Serve it turned upside down, with the apples on top – it's great with custard.

you will need

preparation time *20 minutes*

cooking time *40-50 minutes*

2-3 large dessert apples, peeled, cored and quartered

150g (5½oz) butter, plus a knob for frying

90g (3¼oz) demerara sugar

2 tbsp golden syrup

115g (4oz) caster sugar

2 eggs, beaten

150g (5½oz) self-raising flour

1 tsp ground cinnamon

zest of 1 lemon

2 tbsp milk

tub of custard to serve (for home-made custard, follow the instructions for coffee custard sauce on page 146, omitting the coffee)

1 Pre-heat the oven to 200°C/ 400°F/gas 6. Generously butter a 20cm (8in) square baking tin.

2 Heat the knob of butter in a frying-pan and fry the apples gently until they are just tender. Set aside to cool.

3 Melt 25g (1oz) of the butter with the demerara sugar and golden syrup and stir until the sugar has dissolved. Pour the syrup into the greased baking tin. Lay the apples on top.

4 Cream together the remaining butter and caster sugar until light and fluffy. Slowly beat in the eggs; then fold in the flour, cinnamon and lemon zest. Add the milk to soften.

5 Spoon the mix carefully over the apples and bake for 40-50 minutes until firm to the touch and golden.

to serve

Turn out the sponge on to a board, divide into 6 portions and serve with warm custard.

chapter three
menus for six to
eight and more

springtime surprise

serves 8

pistou salad

lemony roast chicken
with crème fraîche and
crispy bacon sauce

rhubarb tart

Bring a refreshing flavour of spring to your cooking with the zingy tastes that abound in this menu. Make the most of fresh young vegetables in the pistou salad, relish the lemon flavour of the roast chicken and, finally, indulge in the luscious rhubarb dessert.

Shopping list

450g (1lb) red onions
1 small onion
1 bunch spring onions
3 plum or salad tomatoes
55g (2oz) salad leaves (e.g. spinach and rocket)
1 cos or romaine lettuce
1.8kg (4lb) small new potatoes
225g (8oz) fine French beans
650g (1lb 7oz) rhubarb
3 lemons
1 bunch fresh tarragon
2 x 1.6-1.8kg (3½-4lb) chickens
8 rashers unsmoked, rindless back bacon
300ml (10fl oz) good-quality chicken stock (see page 10)
4 eggs
300ml (10fl oz) crème fraîche or soured cream
300ml (10fl oz) milk
300ml (10fl oz) double cream
450g (1lb) frozen garden peas
115g (4oz) unsalted butter
block of parmesan cheese, fresh
1 jar small globe artichokes in oil
1 jar or can stoned black olives
1 jar pesto sauce (for home-made see page 176)
1 jar redcurrant jelly
4 tbsp cooking oil
125ml (4fl oz) olive oil
125ml (4fl oz) groundnut oil
125ml (4fl oz) balsamic vinegar
200g (7oz) caster sugar
350g (12oz) shortcrust pastry (see page 8)
25g (1oz) cornflour
2 vanilla pods
crusty loaf

Prepare ahead

The day before
Pickle the red onions
Make the pastry cream, cool and refrigerate it
Boil and peel the new potatoes for the main course
Blind bake the pastry case

On the day

2-3 hours before guests arrive
Prepare the salad ingredients but do not cook the new potatoes
Assemble the rhubarb tart to the end of step 3, 'Finishing the tart'

1 hour before guests arrive
Put the rhubarb tart in the oven
Put the chicken in the oven

30 minutes before guests arrive
Put the new potatoes for the salad on to boil
Assemble the ingredients for cooking the main course vegetables

Just before sitting down to eat
Halve the salad potatoes and assemble the pistou salad

Between the starter and main course
Sauté the new potatoes
Make the crispy bacon sauce
Cook the peas with lettuce

Between the main course and pudding
Glaze the rhubarb tart

pistou salad

Pistou is traditionally a French soup but here the ingredients are transformed into a tasty warm salad. With so many fresh vegetables, it makes a healthy starter.

you will need

preparation time
20 minutes plus 1-2 hours marinating for the pickled onions

cooking time
35-40 minutes

450g (1lb) red onions
125ml (4fl oz) olive oil
125ml (4fl oz) groundnut oil

125ml (4fl oz) balsamic vinegar
juice of 1 lemon
salt and pepper
12 small new potatoes
225g (8oz) French beans
6 small globe artichokes, preserved in oil or dressing
3 plum or salad tomatoes
4 tbsp pesto sauce, ready-made or home-made (see page 176)

½ bunch spring onions, sliced
16 black olives, stoned and halved
55g (2oz) salad leaves such as spinach and rocket
parmesan flakes
crusty bread, to serve

1 Cut the red onions into 6 or 8 wedges, making sure that each wedge has some root to hold the layers of the onion together. Bring a pan of water to the boil, add the onions and cook for 1-2 minutes.

2 Meanwhile, warm together the oils, balsamic vinegar and a squeeze of lemon juice. When the onions are ready, drain off the liquid and add the onions to the vinegar mix, keeping them off the heat. Season with salt and pepper.

3 Marinate the onions, stirring them occasionally, for at least 1-2 hours. Drain the marinade liquid and reserve.

4 Boil the new potatoes for 10 minutes or until just soft, then drain and halve. Season and add the juice of ½ lemon.

5 Gently warm the pickled onion wedges in 4 tbsp of the reserved onion marinade.

6 Blanch the beans in boiling water for 1 minute, then drain and refresh them in iced water.

7 Quarter the artichokes and cut each tomato into 8 wedges.

8 To make the dressing for the salad, thin the pesto sauce with 3-4 tbsp of the onion marinade.

9 Mix the spring onions and olives, adding the salad leaves at the last minute. Season and spoon the dressing on top. Toss the salad, divide between the serving plates and top with fresh parmesan flakes. Serve with plenty of crusty bread.

lemony roast chicken
with crème fraîche and crispy bacon sauce

The addition of lemon juice and crème fraîche sauce enhanced with crispy bacon and tarragon brings the flavours of spring to a classic roast. New potatoes are given a modern twist – sautéed then sprinkled with tarragon – while serving peas with lettuce revives an old favourite.

you will need
preparation time *20 minutes*
cooking time *1 hour 40 minutes*

for the roast chicken
2 x 1.6-1.8kg (3½-4lb) chickens
2 lemons
salt and pepper
1-2 tbsp cooking oil

for the sauce
8 rashers unsmoked, rindless back bacon
300ml (10fl oz) chicken stock (see page 10)
300ml (10fl oz) crème fraîche or soured cream
salt and pepper
2 tsp chopped fresh tarragon

for the potatoes
1.5kg (3lb 5oz) new potatoes
2 tbsp cooking oil
55g (2oz) butter
salt and pepper
1 tsp chopped fresh tarragon

for the peas and lettuce
25g (1oz) butter
1 small onion, sliced
450g (1lb) frozen peas
1 cos or romaine lettuce, leaves washed and roughly torn
salt and pepper

roasting the chicken
1 Pre-heat the oven to 200°C/400°F/gas 6.
2 Season the chickens with salt and pepper. Halve the lemons and rub, cut side down, over the chickens.
3 Heat the oil in a large roasting tin on the hob. Add the chickens and seal on each side until golden brown. Sit the birds in the tin and squeeze the lemon halves over the top to impart a good lemon flavour.
4 Roast in the pre-heated oven for 1½ hours or until cooked. Remove and set aside to rest on a carving plate. Pour off any fat from the roasting tin and save the lemony chicken juices.
5 Cut each chicken into generous pieces. Keep warm in the oven.

making the sauce
1 Cut the bacon into thin strips, having trimmed any fat, and dry-fry until cooked.
2 Pour the stock into a saucepan and boil to reduce by half. Add the crème fraîche and season.
3 Add the lemon liquid saved from the roasting tin to the stock mix and blitz with a hand-held blender to give a smooth, light finish. Stir in the tarragon and bacon.

cooking the sautéed potatoes
1 Cook the new potatoes in boiling water until they are tender. Allow them to cool, then peel off the skins and halve each potato.
2 Heat the oil and butter in a frying-pan and, once frothy, add the potato halves. Divide into manageable batches, season with salt and pepper and sauté for 4-5 minutes on a high heat until crispy and golden.
3 Remove from the pan and place in a warmed serving dish. Sprinkle with the chopped tarragon.

cooking the peas and lettuce
1 Melt the butter in a saucepan, add the onion and sauté for 3 minutes.
2 Add the peas and season to taste. Stir then cover and simmer for 5 minutes until the peas are tender.
3 Add the lettuce, stir and cook for a further 2 minutes until wilted. Drain off any excess liquid.

to serve
Place one or two chicken pieces on each plate and pour the sauce over them. Serve with the sautéed new potatoes and peas and lettuce.

2 Pre-heat the oven to 220°C/425°F/ gas 7.
3 Line the chilled pastry with greaseproof paper and baking beans and bake blind for 10-15 minutes. Remove the paper and beans and bake for a further 10 minutes until golden and crispy. Remove from the oven and leave to cool.

making the pastry cream
1 Whisk the egg yolks, sugar, salt and cornflour in a bowl.
2 In a pan, bring the milk and vanilla pods to the boil. Remove the pods, halve them lengthways and scrape the seeds into the milk. Whisk the boiling milk into the egg mixture.
3 Pour the mix back into the pan and stir over a medium heat until it has the consistency of thick custard. Remove from the heat and stir in the cream and butter.
4 Strain the pastry cream into a bowl and cover with plastic wrap. Chill overnight.

finishing the tart
1 Pre-heat the oven to 200°C/400°F/ gas 6.
2 Spoon the pastry cream into the prepared case and level off the top.
3 Cut the rhubarb into 2cm (¾in) pieces. Pat dry with kitchen paper, then lightly roll the rhubarb in the sugar. Arrange upright on top of the pastry cream in a single, tightly packed layer.
4 Bake for 35-40 minutes or until the rhubarb is just soft.
5 Remove the tart from the oven and leave to stand for 10-15 minutes. Remove the flan ring and allow to cool slightly on a wire rack.
6 Using a pastry brush, cover the surface of the rhubarb with the melted redcurrant jelly to give the tart a shiny glaze. Serve within 2 hours with double cream.

rhubarb tart

This is a truly seductive pudding – juicy rhubarb nestling on rich pastry cream in a crisp pastry case.

you will need
preparation time *30 minutes*
cooking time *50 minutes*

for the pastry case
350g (12oz) shortcrust pastry (see page 8)

for the pastry cream
4 egg yolks
85g (3oz) caster sugar
small pinch of salt
25g (1oz) cornflour
300ml (10fl oz) milk
2 vanilla pods, split

2 tbsp double cream
25g (1oz) unsalted butter

for the tart topping
650g (1½lb) fresh pink rhubarb, washed and trimmed
115g (4oz) caster sugar
3-4 tbsp redcurrant jelly, melted
double cream, to serve

preparing the pastry case
1 Roll the pastry on a floured surface to 3mm (⅛in) thick and use to line a buttered 23cm (9in) loose-based flan tin. Trim any excess pastry from the edges and chill for 20 minutes.

outdoor entertaining

serves 12

melon and tomato soup

blackened chicken
with aubergines and tomatoes,
corn cobs and baked potatoes

baked orange tart

This light summertime feast is ideal for serving on a hot day. A cold soup makes a refreshing starter, while spicy chicken, baked potatoes and corn-on-the-cob are perfect barbecue partners. To finish, enjoy a tangy orange tart with whipped cream – a delectable pudding that can be made the day before, leaving you more time to savour the sunshine.

Shopping list

1.3kg (3lb) ripe plum or salad tomatoes
12 firm plum tomatoes
3 aubergines
4 corn cobs
8 spring onions
1 cucumber
12 baking potatoes
1 ogen or charentais melon
5 oranges
2 garlic cloves
2 bunches fresh basil leaves
12 chicken breasts, skin left on
300ml (10fl oz) whipping cream
150ml (5fl oz) milk
unsalted butter
2 eggs
ciabatta bread
225g (8oz) white breadcrumbs
175g (6oz) shortcrust pastry (see page 8)
55g (2oz) plain sponge cake crumbs
2 x 400g cans red pimento peppers
600ml (1 pint) ready-made vegetable stock
450ml (16fl oz) olive oil
cooking oil
100ml (3½fl oz) red wine vinegar
350ml (12fl oz) white wine vinegar
garlic powder
onion powder or granules
cumin
cayenne
paprika
white pepper
8 tbsp honey
70g (2½ oz) caster sugar
icing sugar

Prepare ahead

The day before

Make the baked orange tarts
Make the melon and tomato soup and chill in the fridge

On the day

4 hours before guests arrive

Make the marinade for the aubergines and tomatoes, grill the aubergines and tomatoes, then put them into the marinade and leave in the fridge
Make the orange rings in syrup, if serving

1-2 hours before guests arrive

Make the dressing for the aubergines and tomatoes
Scrub the potatoes and put them in the oven (to be finished on the barbecue later)
Mix spices together and blend the oil and butter for the chicken

30 minutes before guests arrive

Light the barbecue so the coals are hot by the time you want to start cooking

Just before starting the barbecue

Garnish the soup
Rub the chicken all over with the spices and oil
Prepare the corn cobs
Take the potatoes out of the oven and wrap in foil

Between the starter and main course

Warm the orange tarts in a medium oven

Between the main course and pudding

Whip the cream and sprinkle icing sugar on the tarts

Tip The soup keeps very well when chilled so you can make it in large quantities. If it has to stand out in the sun for a long time, add a few ice cubes. This will keep it chilled without diluting it too much.

melon and tomato soup

The main ingredients in this chilled soup are melon and ripe tomatoes, but the flavour of fresh basil is clearly apparent. This light starter is quick to make.

you will need
preparation time
15 minutes

for the stock
1.3kg (3lb) ripe plum or salad tomatoes
1 ogen or charentais melon
2 x 400g cans red pimento peppers
1 cucumber
20-24 fresh basil leaves

600ml (1 pint) ready-made vegetable stock, cold
225g (8oz) fresh white breadcrumbs
2 tsp caster sugar (optional)

for the soup
100ml (3½fl oz) red wine vinegar
2 garlic cloves
300ml (10fl oz) olive oil
2 tsp caster sugar

salt and pepper

to serve
ciabatta loaf plus butter
basil leaves, to garnish

1 Drain the pimento peppers, then skin and deseed the tomatoes. Skin, deseed and roughly chop the melon and cucumber.

2 Blitz all the stock ingredients together in a food processor until almost smooth. (You may need to do this in batches.) If the tomatoes are not very ripe, add 2 tsp caster sugar to sweeten them. Set aside.
3 Blitz the vinegar, garlic, olive oil and sugar together in a food processor until well blended. Season the mixture and stir into the stock.
4 Push the mix through a metal sieve, then check the seasoning.
5 Chill in the fridge for at least 3 hours before serving with ciabatta bread and butter and a garnish of basil.

blackened chicken
with aubergines, corn cobs and baked potatoes

This dish is called blackened chicken as the spices give the chicken a black finish. Slices of aubergine and halved tomatoes are marinated and cooked over the coals. Corn-on-the-cob and jacket potatoes complete this mouthwatering course.

you will need

preparation time *10 minutes for the chicken; 5 minutes plus 2-3 hours marinating for the aubergines and tomatoes*

cooking time *15-20 minutes for the chicken; 15-20 minutes for the aubergines and tomatoes; 10-15 minutes for the corn cobs; 1¼ hours for the potatoes*

for the chicken

12 chicken breasts, skin on
2 tbsp salt
3 tsp garlic powder
3 tsp freshly ground black pepper
2 tsp ground white pepper
2 tsp onion powder or granules
2 tsp cumin
1 tsp cayenne pepper
1 tsp paprika
2 tbsp oil
55g (2oz) unsalted butter, softened

for the aubergines and tomatoes

3 aubergines, thickly sliced
12 plum tomatoes, halved

8 tbsp honey
350ml (12fl oz) white wine vinegar
salt and pepper
150ml (5fl oz) olive oil plus extra for brushing
8 spring onions, finely sliced

for the corn cobs

4 corn cobs, cut into 3 pieces each
knobs of butter, melted
salt and pepper

for the baked potatoes

12 baking potatoes, scrubbed
butter, to serve

cooking the chicken

1 Mix all the spices together in a bowl. Coat the chicken breasts with the spices to give a good even covering.
2 Blend the oil and butter together and brush over the chicken breasts. Place the chicken on the barbecue for 15-20 minutes, turning over halfway through cooking, until blackened on both sides.

grilling the aubergines and tomatoes

1 Pre-heat the grill to hot.
2 Boil the honey, 250ml (9fl oz) water and vinegar in a pan, then remove from the heat.
3 Season the aubergine slices and tomato halves with salt and pepper, then brush with olive oil on all sides.
4 Grill the aubergines and tomatoes until coloured but not quite tender. (You may need to do this in batches.) Sit the warm vegetables in the honey marinade and leave for 2-3 hours.
5 Drain the vegetables, reserving the marinade. Place the vegetables on the barbecue and cook for 15-20 minutes until tender.
6 Whisk 150ml (5fl oz) honey marinade with 150ml (5fl oz) olive oil. Stir in the spring onions and pour over the cooked vegetables before serving.

barbecuing the corn cobs

1 Blanch the corn pieces in boiling water for 4 minutes, drain then toss in a little butter and season.
2 Barbecue for 10-15 minutes, turning occasionally. The corn is ready when slightly charred. Serve with more butter and seasoning.

baking the potatoes

1 Pre-heat the oven to 160°C/325°F/gas 3.
2 Bake the potatoes for 1 hour or until tender.
3 Wrap the potatoes in foil and place in the barbecue coals for 10-15 minutes to absorb the smoky flavour. Serve with plenty of butter.

Recipe option

orange rings in syrup
As an optional extra to serve with the orange tart, make these delicious orange rings in syrup.

6-8 oranges

250g (9oz) caster sugar

1 Put the sugar and 300ml (10fl oz) water in a pan and boil until syrupy. Remove from the heat and leave to cool.
2 Peel and pith the oranges, then slice into rings and cover with the syrup. Chill for at least 1 hour before serving.

baked orange tart

This simple pudding has a distinctive zesty orange taste. The recipe makes one 20cm (8in) tart which serves 6-8, but you can make an extra tart if you have more guests.

you will need
preparation time *25 minutes*
cooking time *40-45 minutes*

175g (6oz) shortcrust pastry (see page 8)
zest of 2 oranges, finely grated
55g (2oz) caster sugar
55g (2oz) plain sponge cake crumbs
25g (1oz) unsalted butter, diced
150ml (5fl oz) milk
150ml (5fl oz) fresh orange juice, squeezed from 2-3 oranges
2 eggs, separated

to serve
orange slices
icing sugar for sprinkling
300ml (10fl oz) whipping cream

1 Pre-heat the oven to 180°C/350°F/gas 4.
2 Roll out the pastry thinly and use it to line a 20cm (8in) loose-bottomed flan tin.
3 In a large bowl, mix the orange zest with the sugar until the white granules take on an orange tinge. Add the cake crumbs and the butter.

4 Warm the milk and pour over the crumb mixture. Stir until the butter has melted, then add the orange juice and egg yolks.
5 Whisk the egg whites to a soft peak and gently fold into the mix.
6 Pour the mixture into the pastry case and bake in the oven for 40-45 minutes until light brown and set.

to serve
1 Peel one of the zested oranges and slice it thinly and horizontally. Lay the slices decoratively across the centre of the tart. Leave the tart to rest for at least 20 minutes.
2 Meanwhile, whip the cream until it forms soft peaks. Sprinkle the tart with icing sugar just before serving it with the whipped cream.

tropical barbecue

serves 8

sweet potato wedges
with tomato and red onion salsa

grilled tuna steaks
with vegetable kebabs and bean salad

glazed pineapple
with honeyed mascarpone and
passion fruit dips

Eating outdoors is one of the great pleasures of summer and cooking outside can be just as fun. Every course of this menu is enhanced by open grilling – sweet potatoes to start, followed by tuna with vegetable kebabs, while for dessert – glazed pineapple slices.

Shopping list

650g (1lb 7oz) sweet potatoes
1 red onion; 1 white onion
2 plum tomatoes; 32 cherry tomatoes
1 gem lettuce
6 garlic cloves
3 courgettes
8 chestnut mushrooms; 8 button mushrooms
1 red pepper
1 yellow pepper
1 large avocado
pack of fresh parsley
pack of fresh basil
pack of fresh dill
pack of fresh coriander
2 large ripe pineapples
2 tbsp grated fresh root ginger
2 lemons, 4 limes
6 passion fruits
8 tuna steaks, about 140g (5oz) each
300g (10oz) mascarpone
300g (10oz) crème fraîche
4 tbsp natural yoghurt
6 tbsp double cream
420g can red kidney beans
410g can black-eyed beans
1 tsp sugar
2 tbsp icing sugar
2 tbsp dark muscovado sugar
4 tbsp clear honey
2 tbsp tomato ketchup
12 tbsp olive oil
1 pickled gherkin
½ tsp chilli sauce
1 tsp paprika
1 tsp cayenne
6 tbsp brandy
16 wooden or metal skewers

Prepare ahead

On the day

2-3 hours before guests arrive

Slice the sweet potatoes and leave to marinate in their spicy coating

Prepare the tomato and red onion salsa and refrigerate

Marinate the tuna steaks

1 hour before sitting down to eat

Prepare the vegetable kebabs and refrigerate

Prepare the bean salad and refrigerate

30 minutes before sitting down to eat

Prepare and marinate the pineapple slices

Prepare the honeyed mascarpone and passion fruit dip, and refrigerate

Barbecue the sweet potato wedges

Between the starter and main course

Barbecue the vegetable kebabs and the tuna steaks

Between the main course and pudding

Barbecue the pineapple slices

Cook's notes

The minimum time given to marinate the sweet potatoes is 30 minutes. However, their flavour improves greatly if you leave them to marinate for longer. If there is any marinade left in the mixing bowl after you have put the potatoes on the barbecue, spoon it over the wedges while you cook them.

sweet potato wedges
with tomato and red onion salsa

The nutty flavour of sweet potato is really brought out by barbecuing. As a bonus, the spicy coating of the potatoes becomes delightfully crisp.

you will need

preparation time
15 minutes plus
30 minutes marinating

cooking time
15-20 minutes

for the sweet potatoes
650g (1lb 7oz) sweet
potatoes, scrubbed
1 tsp paprika
1 tsp cayenne pepper
2 tbsp tomato ketchup
1 tsp salt
2 tbsp dark muscovado
sugar
juice of 1 lemon
4 tbsp natural yoghurt

for the salsa
2 plum tomatoes
1 red onion, finely chopped
1 pickled gherkin, chopped
2 tbsp chopped fresh parsley
1/2 tsp chilli sauce
salt and pepper

1 In a large bowl, mix together the paprika, cayenne pepper, tomato ketchup, sugar, salt and lemon juice. Then add the yoghurt and stir well.
2 Cut the sweet potatoes into chunky wedges about 7.5cm (3in) long.
3 Put the potato wedges into the spicy paste and mix until they are well coated. Put in the fridge and leave them to marinate for 30 minutes.
4 To make the salsa, cut a cross into the stalk end of the tomatoes and put them briefly into boiling water. Take them out, peel and dice the flesh. Mix with the onion, gherkin, parsley and chilli sauce. Season to taste.
5 Put the sweet potato wedges on a hot barbecue and cook for 15-20 minutes, turning occasionally, until crispy on the outside and tender in the middle. Serve straight away with the spicy tomato and red onion salsa.

grilled tuna steaks
with vegetable kebabs and bean salad

Barbecuing tuna is one of the best ways to cook it. It ensures that the outside of the steaks browns really fast, while the inside stays pink. Grilling vegetables is healthy – it preserves their goodness, as well as their flavour and crunch.

you will need

preparation time *10 minutes for the tuna plus at least 2 hours for marinating; 15 minutes for the vegetable kebabs; 15 minutes for the bean salad*

cooking time *5-10 minutes for the tuna steaks; 10 minutes for the vegetable kebabs*

for the tuna steaks

8 tuna steaks, about 140g (5oz) each
3 tbsp olive oil
4 garlic cloves, crushed
2 tbsp chopped fresh basil
2 tbsp chopped fresh dill
juice and zest of 1 lime
salt and pepper
2 limes, cut into quarters

for the vegetable kebabs

3 courgettes, cut into 2.5cm (1in) pieces
8 chestnut mushrooms, halved
8 button mushrooms
1 red pepper and 1 yellow pepper, deseeded, cut into 2.5cm (1in) squares
32 cherry tomatoes
4 tbsp olive oil

2 garlic cloves, crushed
salt and pepper

for the bean salad

420g can red kidney beans
410g can black-eyed beans
1 large avocado, peeled and sliced
1 onion, finely chopped
1 gem lettuce

for the lime and coriander dressing

juice of 1 lime
5 tbsp olive oil
3 tbsp chopped fresh coriander
salt and pepper
1 tsp sugar

grilling the tuna

1 To make the marinade, mix together the olive oil, crushed garlic, three-quarters of the chopped herbs, lime juice and zest and seasoning in a large, shallow bowl.
2 Add the tuna steaks and turn until they are well-coated. Cover with plastic wrap and put in the fridge to marinate for at least 2 hours.
3 Take the tuna steaks out of the marinade, reserving the excess for

basting. Brush a little of the marinade on to the grill of the barbecue to help prevent the tuna steaks from sticking to it.
4 Cook the steaks over a hot barbecue for about 5 minutes on each side, basting frequently.
5 Serve the steaks immediately, garnished with the rest of the fresh herbs and quarters of lime.

grilling the vegetable kebabs

1 Mix together the olive oil, crushed garlic and salt and pepper.
2 Put the vegetables into a shallow bowl, then pour the olive oil mixture over them and turn until they are well-coated.
3 Thread the vegetables on to skewers, putting different vegetable pieces on one after the other so that each skewer has a selection.
4 Brush the barbecue grill with oil. Cook the vegetable skewers for 8-10 minutes, turning regularly and basting with any remaining marinade until the vegetables are tender and slightly charred at the edges.

making the bean salad

1 Drain and thoroughly rinse the beans. Peel and slice the avocado and mix with the chopped onion and beans.
2 Separate and wash the gem lettuce leaves, then tear them up coarsely.
3 Combine all the dressing ingredients together and whisk until blended. Pour over the beans, avocado and onion and mix.
4 Toss the bean mixture and lettuce leaves together, spoon into a large bowl and serve.

glazed pineapple
with two creamy dips

When fruit is barbecued, its natural sugars caramelize, turning golden brown. In this recipe, the pineapple is soaked in brandy before it is grilled, and the combination of sugar and alcohol turns into a scrumptious caramel coating.

you will need

preparation time *10 minutes plus 30 minutes for marinating*

cooking time *5 minutes*

for the glazed pineapple

2 large ripe pineapples, peeled and cut into 2.5cm (1in) slices

2 tbsp grated root ginger

6 tbsp brandy

for the honeyed mascarpone dip

300g (10oz) mascarpone

6 tbsp double cream

4 tbsp clear honey

zest of 1 lemon

for the passion fruit dip

300g (10oz) crème fraîche

2 tbsp icing sugar

seeds and juice of 6 large passion fruits

glazing the pineapple

1 Put the pineapple slices in a dish and scatter the grated ginger over the top.

2 Pour the brandy over the pineapple and ginger; cover and refrigerate for at least 30 minutes.

3 Remove the slices from the marinade and grill them on the barbecue. Reserve the marinade to add to the honeyed mascarpone.

4 Cook the pineapple slices for about 5 minutes, turning occasionally, until golden brown on both sides. Serve while still warm.

sweetening the mascarpone

1 In a large mixing bowl, beat the mascarpone until soft. Stir in the cream, honey and lemon zest.

2 Mix 4 tbsp of the pineapple marinade into the honeyed mascarpone before spooning into a serving bowl.

mixing the passion fruit dip

1 Beat together all the ingredients until well-mixed.

2 Spoon into a serving bowl and serve with the pineapple slices.

lunch alfresco

serves 6-8

parsley and onion tart
with new potato salad

honey mustard sausages
Mediterranean picnic loaf

crumbly apple cake

Picnic food has to travel well and be kept cool in transit – a rigid cool box chilled with frozen ice packs is ideal. In this alfresco lunch, the savoury tart, potato salad, picnic loaf, sausages and cake are robust enough to transport easily, and substantial enough to satisfy appetites sharpened by a day in the fresh air. Remember to take plenty of chilled drinks and flasks of tea and coffee.

Shopping list

900g (2lb) new potatoes
25g (1oz) young spinach leaves
mixed salad leaves
4 large onions
225g (8oz) shallots
3 plum tomatoes
350g (12oz) cooking apples
1 garlic clove
1 bunch flatleaf parsley
225g (8oz) cooked chicken breast
900g (2lb) chipolata sausages
85g (3oz) sliced salami
milk
300ml (10fl oz) double cream
300ml (10fl oz) single cream
175g (6oz) unsalted butter
140g (5oz) mozzarella cheese
2 tbsp fresh parmesan
2 eggs
1 large crusty loaf
450g (1lb) puff pastry (see page 9)
2 tbsp runny honey
2 tbsp wholegrain mustard
85g (3oz) artichokes in oil
55g (2oz) green olives, stoned
300ml (10fl oz) mayonnaise (see page 187)
4-5 tbsp vinaigrette (see page 22)
olive oil, cooking oil
3 tbsp pesto sauce (see page 176)
225g (8oz) self-raising flour
cinnamon and nutmeg
115g (4oz) soft brown sugar
1-2 tbsp demerara sugar

Prepare ahead

The day before

Assemble the picnic loaf, wrap tightly in plastic wrap or double thickness greaseproof paper and store in the fridge

Make the crumbly apple cake, allow to cool and store in an airtight container

Make the parsley and onion tart, cover and store in the fridge

On the day

In the morning

Make the potato salad and store in an airtight container

Bake the honey mustard sausages, leave to cool and wrap in foil

Packing the hamper

Pack all the food carefully into firm plastic containers with lids and then into a basket, box or picnic hamper with frozen ice packs to keep everything cool

Other essentials to take on a picnic

Rug to sit on and tablecloth to spread out

Plates, glasses and cutlery – preferably disposable ones

Napkins and wet-wipes

Plastic bag for rubbish

Insect repellent and wasp decoy

If you're taking wine, don't forget the corkscrew!

Drain and refresh in cold water, then chop coarsely.
2 Warm the oil and butter; add the onions, shallots and garlic. Cook until softened, without colouring. Remove from heat and allow to cool.
3 Meanwhile, beat together the cream, parmesan and eggs. Season well.
4 Once the onion mixture is cooled, mix it into the eggy cream. Then add the parsley and seasoning.

cooking the tart
1 Pre-heat the oven to 200°C/400°F/gas 6.
2 Spoon the filling into the case and bake for 30-35 minutes or until slightly set.
3 Remove the tart from the oven and allow to cool before taking it out of the tin.

parsley and onion tart
with new potato salad

Treat this crisp-cased parsley and onion tart as a starter – it's delicious with new potatoes in a creamy dressing.

parsley and onion tart
you will need
preparation time
30 minutes plus 10 minutes cooling
cooking time
15-20 minutes for the case; 6 minutes for the filling; 30-35 minutes to finish

450g (1lb) puff pastry (see page 9)
1 bunch flatleaf parsley
3 large onions, sliced
225g (8oz) shallots, sliced
1 tbsp olive oil
25g (1oz) unsalted butter
1 garlic clove, crushed
300ml (10fl oz) double cream
2 heaped tbsp grated fresh parmesan
2 eggs, beaten
salt and pepper

making the case
1 Pre-heat the oven to 200°C/400°F/gas 6.
2 Roll out the pastry thinly on a lightly floured surface.

Use it to line a 23cm (9in) flan tin. Drape the surplus over the edges without trimming it. Leave in the fridge for 10-15 minutes.
3 Line the pastry case with greaseproof paper and baking beans and bake for 15-20 minutes, or until golden.
4 Remove the paper and beans, and trim the excess pastry from around the edges of the tin. Leave the pastry case in the tin.

making the filling
1 Pick the parsley from the stalks and blanch in boiling water for 45 seconds.

new potato salad
you will need
preparation time
10 minutes
cooking time
10-12 minutes

900g (2lb) new potatoes
1 large onion, finely chopped
4-5 tbsp basic vinaigrette (see page 22)
salt and pepper
300ml (10fl oz) mayonnaise (see page 187)

1 Lightly scrub the potatoes and cook in boiling water for 10-12 minutes or until tender. Drain. Quarter while still hot.
2 Put the potatoes and onions in a bowl and add the vinaigrette. Season.
3 When cold, bind with the mayonnaise.

savoury treats
sausages and Mediterranean picnic loaf

Chipolata sausages coated with a honey mustard glaze are irresistible to adults and children alike. A hollowed-out picnic loaf packed with layers of savoury fillings makes a welcome change from sandwiches and is easy to transport. Salad leaves go well with both.

home-made pesto sauce

55g (2oz) pine nuts
150ml (5fl oz) olive oil
1 garlic clove, crushed
1 large bunch fresh basil, chopped
salt and pepper

1 Put the pine nuts in a pan and sauté them in the olive oil until lightly coloured. Leave to cool.
2 Add the garlic, basil and seasoning. Blend into a purée.

honey mustard sausages
you will need

preparation time *5 minutes*
cooking time *30-40 minutes*

2-4 tsp cooking oil
900g (2lb) chipolata sausages
2 tbsp runny honey
2 tbsp wholegrain mustard
salt and pepper

1 Pre-heat the oven to 200°C/ 400°F/gas 6.
2 Lightly grease a roasting tin with the cooking oil. Put the sausages in the tin.
3 Mix the honey and mustard together in a small bowl. Brush or spoon the mixture over the sausages. Add a little seasoning and turn the sausages to ensure an even coating.
4 Bake the sausages in the pre-heated oven for 30-40 minutes or until cooked through.

Mediterranean picnic loaf
you will need

preparation time *20 minutes*
cooking time *20 minutes*

1 large crusty loaf
3 tbsp pesto sauce (home-made (see above) or ready-made)
225g (8oz) cooked chicken breast
25g (1oz) young spinach leaves, finely shredded
3 plum tomatoes, sliced
2 tbsp olive oil
salt and pepper
140g (5oz) mozzarella cheese, sliced
85g (3oz) artichokes in oil, drained
85g (3oz) sliced salami
55g (2oz) green olives, stoned
15g (½oz) butter, softened

1 Slice off the base of the loaf, about 1cm (½in) from the bottom and set aside. Using a dessertspoon or your fingers, scoop out the inside of the loaf leaving a 1cm (½in) thick wall. Discard the insides. Spread the pesto sauce over the hollowed-out loaf.
2 Thickly slice the chicken and place half inside the loaf with half the spinach leaves. Add half the tomatoes and drizzle over half the olive oil. Season lightly.
3 Add layers of cheese and artichokes, top with the remaining tomatoes and season. Next, lay the salami and olives on top, and add the remaining chicken and spinach. Drizzle over the rest of the olive oil and season.
4 Butter the base and replace it on the loaf. Wrap the loaf tightly in cling film and chill in the fridge overnight. To serve, unwrap and cut into generous wedges.

Tip For added flavour and texture, you can substitute 85g (3oz) chopped dates and 85g (3oz) chopped walnuts for 175g (6oz) of the apple. Simply add these to the other ingredients with the apple in step 3.

crumbly apple cake

With juicy chunks of apple in a moist sponge cake, sprinkled with sugar to give a crunchy topping, this fresh-flavoured cake will quickly become a favourite.

you will need

preparation time *10 minutes*

cooking time *40 minutes*

350g (12oz) cooking apples

225g (8oz) self-raising flour

pinch of salt

pinch of cinnamon

pinch of nutmeg

115g (4oz) butter, roughly chopped

115g (4oz) soft brown sugar

2-3 tbsp milk

1-2 tbsp demerara sugar

300ml (10fl oz) single cream, to serve

1 Pre-heat the oven to 180°C/350°F/gas 4. Lightly grease a 23cm (9in) flan tin or sandwich tin and sit it on a baking sheet.

2 Sift the flour, salt and spices into a bowl and rub in the butter until the mixture resembles fine breadcrumbs.

3 Peel, core and finely chop the apples and mix them with the soft brown sugar.

4 Stir into the flour mixture and beat in enough milk to form a soft but not sticky batter.

5 Spoon the mixture into the prepared tin and spread it evenly around the sides. Sprinkle with the demerara sugar to give the cake a crunchy topping.

6 Place in the pre-heated oven and bake for 40-45 minutes or until firm to the touch.

7 Cut into slices to serve, with a little single cream poured on top.

picnic treats

serves 8

cheese and onion rolls
Lebanese tuna salad
in pitta pockets

cold roast chicken
with chick-pea and new potato salads

raspberry brownies

Apicnic on the first warm day of the year is a joy. With roast chicken, tuna-stuffed pittas, cheese and onion rolls and chick-pea salad, this selection is quick to prepare and tastes delightful. Squidgy chocolate and raspberry brownies sweetly round off the picnic. Take plenty of drinks, too, hot and cold.

Shopping list

- 1 medium onion
- 7 garlic cloves; 1 large garlic clove
- 12 spring onions
- 1 red pepper
- 900g (2lb) new potatoes
- 2.5cm (1in) fresh ginger
- 1 bag of watercress
- small bunch of parsley
- small bunch of coriander
- sprig of mint
- 2 bay leaves
- 175g (6oz) raspberries
- 2 lemons
- 1.8-2.25kg (4-5lb) chicken
- 2 eggs
- 115g (4oz) butter
- 85g (3oz) shredded vegetarian suet
- 175g (6oz) strong cheddar cheese
- 8-16 pitta breads
- 400g can tuna in brine
- 3 x 439g cans of chick-peas
- 55g (2oz) dark bitter chocolate
- 225g (8oz) granulated sugar
- 175g (6oz) self-raising flour
- 55g (2oz) plain flour
- 1 tsp baking powder
- 115g (4oz) chopped nuts
- 2 tbsp tahini
- ½ tsp thyme; ½ tsp dried marjoram
- 1 tsp ground cumin; cayenne pepper
- 150ml (5fl oz) olive oil

Prepare ahead

2 days before

Marinate the chicken

The day before

Make the raspberry brownies, allow to cool completely and put in an airtight container

Make the chick-pea salad and store in a plastic container in the fridge

Make the cheese and onion rolls

Roast the chicken

On the day

1 hour before setting off

Make the potato salad, allow to cool and put in a plastic container

Make the tuna salad and chill in a plastic container in the fridge

15 minutes before setting off

Put the chicken into a cool bag. Pack the rest of the food and cold drinks carefully into a hamper or basket with frozen ice packs to keep everything cool

For other picnic essentials, see page 174

Once you're there

Stuff the pitta pockets with the tuna salad and watercress

4 Brush a little water around the edges of each pastry rectangle.
5 Combine the grated cheese, onion, salt and pepper and scatter this mixture down the centre of each piece of pastry.
6 Roll up the pastry from the long side – like a sausage roll – and slice into 4 or 5 pieces so you have a total of 8 to 10 rolls.
7 Put the rolls, sealed-edge side down, on a baking tray lined with baking parchment or greaseproof paper.
8 Bake for 15-20 minutes until golden and crispy.

Lebanese tuna salad in pitta pockets
you will need
preparation time
15 minutes

---

1 x 400g can tuna chunks in brine
2 tbsp tahini
3 tbsp fresh lemon juice
1 large garlic clove, crushed
good pinch of cayenne pepper
4 tbsp olive oil
4 spring onions, thinly sliced
4 tbsp chopped parsley
salt and pepper
1 bag of watercress
8-16 pitta breads

---

1 Drain the tuna, place in a bowl and break up with a fork. Mix in the tahini, lemon juice, garlic, cayenne, olive oil, parsley and spring onions and season to taste.
2 At the picnic, fill the pittas with 3 tbsp of the tuna salad and a handful of watercress.

neatly packaged savouries

Cheese and onion rolls are so scrumptious they will be gobbled up before you know it, while the pitta pockets make good picnic staples. They hold the fillings well and work perfectly with the Lebanese tuna salad.

cheese and onion rolls
you will need
preparation time
25 minutes
cooking time
15-20 minutes

for the pastry
175g (6oz) self-raising flour
pinch of salt

85g (3oz) shredded vegetarian suet

for the filling
175g (6oz) strong cheddar cheese, grated
1 onion, finely chopped
salt and cayenne pepper

1 Pre-heat the oven to 220°C/425°F/gas 7.

2 Sift the flour and salt and mix in the suet. Add enough cold water (about 5 tbsp) to the sifted mix, a little at a time, to form a pliable dough.
3 Divide the dough in half and roll out each piece into a 30 x 10cm (12 x 4in) rectangle on a floured surface.

cold roast chicken
with chick-pea and new potato salads

Roast chicken is a picnic favourite and here the salad accompaniments are simple yet highly effective. The chick-pea, cumin and coriander salad has a slightly spicy flavour, which is balanced by the freshness of the new potato salad.

Cook's notes

As an alternative, you can serve the roast chicken warm. Marinate the chicken overnight and cook it on the morning of the picnic. Remove it from the oven just before leaving. You will need to carry it in a foil-lined bag to retain the heat and keep it away from any ice packs. Any left-overs must be refrigerated immediately or thrown away.

cold roast chicken
you will need

preparation time *20 minutes*
marinating time *overnight*
cooking time *1 hour 20 minutes*

1.8-2.25kg (4-5lb) chicken
salt and pepper

for the marinade
juice of 1 lemon
6 garlic cloves
2 bay leaves
½ tsp thyme
½ tsp dried marjoram

1 Put all the ingredients for the marinade in a blender and blitz until smooth.
2 Pour the marinade into a large bowl. Add the chicken and roll it around in the marinade so it is well-coated. Then spoon a little marinade inside the body cavity.
3 Leave the chicken in the bowl, cover it with plastic wrap and marinate in the fridge overnight.

4 When you are ready to cook the chicken, pre-heat the oven to 190°C/375°F/gas 5.
5 Place the chicken on a roasting rack in a roasting tin. Season well with salt and pepper and roast for about 1 hour 20 minutes, basting occasionally with the marinade, until the chicken is well cooked.

chick-pea, cumin and coriander salad
you will need

preparation time *20 minutes*
chilling time *overnight*

for the salad
3 x 439g cans of chick-peas, drained and rinsed
1 red pepper, finely chopped
8 spring onions, finely chopped
small bunch of coriander, chopped

for the dressing
2 tbsp lemon juice
1 garlic clove, crushed
1 tsp fresh chopped ginger

1 tsp ground cumin
good pinch cayenne pepper
6 tbsp olive oil

1 In a bowl, combine all the salad ingredients and set aside.
2 Whisk together all the dressing ingredients in a small bowl and pour over the chick-pea salad.
3 Cover with plastic wrap and leave it in the fridge overnight.

new potato salad
you will need

900g (2lb) new potatoes
sprig of mint
3 tbsp olive oil
salt and pepper

1 Bring a pan of water to the boil.
2 Scrub the potatoes and cut in half.
3 Add the potatoes, a pinch of salt and the mint to the pan of boiling water. Cook for 10-12 minutes, then drain.
4 Drizzle with olive oil and season with plenty of pepper. Leave to cool.

raspberry brownies

Dark and delicious, brownies make great sweet treats for picnics. You can make them the day before – they seem to get richer and squidgier overnight!

you will need
preparation time *20 minutes*
cooking time *30 minutes plus 10 minutes to cool*

55g (2oz) dark bitter chocolate, broken into chunks
175g (6oz) raspberries
115g (4oz) butter
2 eggs, beaten
225g (8oz) granulated sugar
55g (2oz) plain flour, sifted
1 tsp baking powder

¼ tsp salt
115g (4oz) chopped nuts – pecans, walnuts or hazelnuts

1 Pre-heat the oven to 180°C/ 350°F/gas 4.
2 Grease and line an 18 x 28cm (7 x 11in) non-stick baking tin with baking parchment. Bring the lining paper well over the rim of the tin.
3 Melt the butter and chocolate in a heatproof bowl over gently simmering water, stirring occasionally.

4 Remove the melted mixture from the heat and stir in all the other ingredients, apart from the raspberries, and mix well. Gently spoon in the raspberries, then pour the mixture into the baking tin and spread it out evenly.
5 Bake in the oven for 30 minutes until the mixture shrinks away from the sides of the tin a little and a knife inserted into the centre comes out clean.
6 Leave to cool for 10 minutes before removing from the tin; then divide into squares. When cold, put in an airtight container lined with greaseproof paper. Don't pack them too tightly or they'll stick together.

midsummer supper

serves 8

prawn cocktail

beef carpaccio
with pesto pasta salad and
chargrilled peppers

brown-sugar pavlova
with raspberries and nectarines

On a sunny day, meals that don't take long to prepare are welcome. This is a menu with unfussy recipes and much of the preparation can be done in advance. The prawn cocktail and the pavlova are re-workings of two classics while beef carpaccio – marinated topside of beef served raw and thinly sliced – is ideal for summer entertaining.

Shopping list

1 large cucumber
1 iceberg lettuce
4 garlic cloves
2 bunches fresh basil
½ bunch fresh thyme
3 red peppers
2 yellow peppers
2 orange peppers
2 lemons
2 nectarines
85g (3oz) raspberries
650-800g (1lb 7oz-1lb 12 oz) cooked prawns
6 eggs
300ml (10fl oz) double or whipping cream
55g (2oz) parmesan
900g (2lb) topside of beef
300ml (10fl oz) dry white wine
600ml (1 pint) olive oil
450g (1lb) pasta spirals
115g (4oz) caster sugar
55g (2oz) soft, light brown sugar
pesto sauce (see page 176)
150ml (5fl oz) balsamic vinegar
5 tbsp soy sauce
5 tbsp Worcestershire sauce
6 tbsp extra virgin olive oil
5 tbsp lemon juice
tomato ketchup
mayonnaise (see page 187)
brandy
vinegar
paprika
black peppercorns
coarse sea salt
cornflour

Prepare ahead

Up to 10 days before
Marinate the beef in the fridge for at least 4 days or a maximum of 10 days

The day before
Make the cocktail sauce and chill in the fridge
Make the pepper salad and store in the fridge
Make the meringue and keep in an airtight container

On the day
In the morning
Make the pasta salad, cover with plastic wrap and store in a cool place
Take the beef out of the marinade, cover and store both in the fridge

2-3 hours before guests arrive
Slice the beef and arrange on a serving plate, cover and store in the fridge
Shred the lettuce and put into iced water
Slice the cucumber, cover and store in the fridge
Assemble the pavlova and keep in a cool place

Just before sitting down to eat
Drain the lettuce and cucumber and assemble the prawn cocktail

Between the starter and main course
Garnish the sliced beef with parmesan shavings and basil leaves

mayonnaise
makes 600ml (1 pint)

3 egg yolks
1 tbsp malt, white wine or balsamic vinegar
1 tsp English or Dijon mustard
salt and pepper
300ml (10fl oz) olive oil
a few drops of lemon juice

1 Beat the egg yolks, wine or vinegar, mustard and seasoning together in a cold, clean bowl with a balloon whisk until they are thoroughly blended.
2 Add the oil a drop at a time, whisking all the time by hand or in a blender. Once it starts to thicken, trickle the remaining oil in faster.
3 Whisk in 1 tsp hot water, and season to taste. Add lemon juice to sharpen the flavour.

prawn cocktail

Prawns coated in a mouthwatering cocktail sauce and served on a bed of crisp lettuce and cucumber make a light and refreshing starter – one that's quick and easy to prepare.

you will need
preparation time
10 minutes

650-800g (1lb 7oz-1lb 12oz) large cooked prawns, shelled, reserving 8 with tails for garnish
1 large cucumber
1 iceberg lettuce, shredded
squeeze of lemon juice
coarse sea salt
paprika for sprinkling
1 lemon, cut into wedges

for the cocktail sauce
2-3 tbsp tomato ketchup
8 tbsp mayonnaise (see above)
1 tbsp lemon juice
1-2 tsp brandy

1 To make the cocktail sauce, whisk the tomato ketchup into the mayonnaise. Stir in the lemon juice and brandy. For a stronger tomato flavour, add more ketchup, a little at a time.
2 Thinly slice the cucumber into rounds.
3 Place the shredded lettuce in a large bowl. Chop 10 prawns and add to the lettuce. Season with coarse sea salt and a squeeze of lemon juice. Add the cocktail sauce to bind the ingredients together.
4 Put enough cucumber slices in a fan-shape to cover the base of the serving glass. Divide the prawn mix between the servings and put on top of the cucumber. Top with cucumber slices. Divide the rest of the shelled prawns between the glasses.

to serve
Place a tailed prawn on top of each serving. Sprinkle a little paprika on top and garnish with a lemon wedge.

beef carpaccio
with pesto pasta salad and chargrilled peppers

Usually served as a starter, this is the perfect centrepiece for a light summery meal. The raw topside of beef absorbs the flavours of a lightly spiced marinade before being sliced wafer thin and served with grilled peppers and a pesto-flavoured pasta salad.

wrap. Store the meat and the marinade separately in the fridge until needed.

to serve
1 Slice the meat very thinly and arrange in a single layer on a serving plate, covering the whole surface.
2 Push the marinade through a sieve to use as a dressing. Chop half the basil leaves and add to the dressing. Brush over the meat, season with pepper and top with parmesan shavings and the rest of the basil leaves.

cooking the pasta salad
1 Bring a large pan of lightly salted water to the boil, add the pasta and cook until *al dente*.
2 Drain the cooked pasta, refresh in cold water and stir in the pesto sauce. Season generously with pepper and refrigerate for at least 1 hour before serving.

cooking the peppers
1 Pre-heat the grill.
2 Halve and deseed all the peppers. Place them cut side down under the grill and cook for 10-15 minutes or until the skin is charred. Remove them from the grill and cover with a clean, damp tea-towel. Allow to cool. Peel off the skins and throw them away. Cut the flesh into thick strips and place in a serving dish.
3 Combine the olive oil and lemon juice in a bowl. Pour over the peppers, cover with plastic wrap and chill in the fridge for at least 1 hour. Sprinkle with pepper just before serving.

you will need
preparation time *10 minutes plus 4-10 days marinating for the beef; 5 minutes for the pasta salad; 15 minutes for the peppers*
cooking time *10-12 minutes for the pasta salad; 5-10 minutes for the peppers*

900g (2lb) topside of beef
1 bunch fresh basil
55g (2oz) fresh parmesan shavings
coarse black pepper

for the marinade
150ml (5fl oz) balsamic vinegar
5 tbsp soy sauce
5 tbsp Worcestershire sauce
4 garlic cloves, chopped
1 bunch fresh basil
½ bunch fresh thyme
15 black peppercorns, crushed
300ml (10fl oz) dry white wine
600ml (1 pint) olive oil
15g (½oz) coarse sea salt

for the pesto pasta salad
450g (1lb) pasta spirals
3-4 tbsp pesto sauce (see page 176)
salt and pepper

for the chargrilled peppers
3 red peppers
2 yellow peppers
2 orange peppers
6 tbsp extra virgin olive oil
4 tbsp lemon juice
pepper

marinating the beef
1 Mix together the marinade ingredients in a large bowl.
2 Trim any fat and sinew off the beef, then roll it in the marinade. Cover and leave in the fridge for at least 4 days to allow time for the flavours to be absorbed. Turn the beef in the marinade daily. (For a stronger flavour, you can leave the beef to marinate in the fridge for up to 10 days.)
3 Remove the meat from the marinade and cover with plastic

brown-sugar pavlova
with raspberries and nectarines

Juicy raspberries and fragrant nectarines combine delightfully with crisp meringue and whipped cream.

you will need

preparation time 15 minutes

cooking time 1 hour

6 egg whites

115g (4oz) caster sugar

55g (2oz) soft, light brown sugar, sieved

1 tsp vinegar

1 tsp cornflour

300ml (10fl oz) double or whipping cream

2 ripe nectarines

85g (3oz) fresh raspberries

1 Pre-heat the oven to 150°C/300°F/gas 2. Line a baking sheet with non-stick baking paper and using a cake tin base, mark out a 20cm (8in) circle.

2 In a large bowl, whisk the egg whites to form soft peaks. Gradually add the sugars, whisking well. Whisk in the vinegar and cornflour with the last of the sugar.

3 Spread the meringue mixture on to the baking paper within the circle, building up the sides slightly. Bake for 1 hour or until pale brown and crisp.

4 Turn off the oven but leave the meringue inside to cool completely. When cool, carefully remove from the baking sheet, peel off the baking paper and place on a serving plate.

5 Halve the nectarines and remove the stones. Thinly slice each half into six. Discard any raspberries that are badly bruised.

6 Whip the cream until it forms soft peaks. Spoon the cream on to the meringue and arrange the raspberries and nectarines on top.

summer buffet

serves 12-16

goat's cheese dips

smoked salmon terrine
with warm green salad

lazy summer puddings

When catering for 12 or more people, it is a good idea to serve finger food or dishes that can be eaten with just a fork. Start with goat's cheese dips and follow with smoked salmon terrine served with a green salad. A simple, but stylish, take on the classic summer pudding makes a refreshing dessert.

Shopping list

2 x 30g packets parsley
1 x 30g packet sorrel
2 tbsp chopped fresh dill
2 bulbs of garlic
2 yellow peppers
4 large carrots
4 sticks celery
6-8 courgettes
450g (1lb) sugar snap peas
2 heads fennel
225g bag baby spinach
2 bunches watercress
6 lemons
900g (2lb) redcurrants, plus a few extra bunches to decorate
900g (2lb) blackcurrants
900g (2lb) raspberries
1-1.5kg (2lb 4oz-3lb 5oz) sliced smoked salmon
300g (10½oz) mild goat's cheese
150ml (5fl oz) soured cream
175g (6oz) unsalted butter
2-3 eggs
3 ciabatta loaves
2 brioche loaves
500g (1lb 2oz) caster sugar
icing sugar
55g (2oz) marinated anchovies
1 heaped tbsp capers
2 tbsp chilli oil
500ml (18fl oz) olive oil
paprika
100ml (3½fl oz) crème de cassis

Prepare ahead

The day before

Make the smoked salmon terrine, weigh it down and refrigerate

On the day

In the morning

Make the dips

2-3 hours before guests arrive

Prepare the crudités
Toast the ciabatta to make the bruschetta
Make the dressing for the warm green salad
Make the lazy summer puddings and frost the redcurrants for decoration

30 minutes before serving the smoked salmon terrine

Blanch the vegetables for the warm green salad
Assemble the salad
Cut the terrine into slices

Just before serving the lazy summer puddings

Decorate with the frosted redcurrants

goat's cheese dips

These two dips use a creamy, mild goat's cheese as a base. The first is inspired by the herby relish, salsa verde; the second is flavoured with the sweetness of yellow peppers.

you will need
preparation time
25 minutes plus chilling
cooking time
15-20 minutes

for the salsa verde dip
30g packet flatleaf parsley
30g packet sorrel
1 garlic clove, crushed
1 heaped tbsp capers
1 tbsp chilli oil

150g (5½oz) goat's cheese
75ml (2½fl oz) soured cream
squeeze of lemon juice
pepper, to taste

for the yellow pepper dip
2 yellow peppers, deseeded and quartered
1 garlic clove, crushed
1 tbsp chilli oil
150g (5½oz) goat's cheese

75ml (2½fl oz) soured cream
squeeze of lemon juice
pinch of paprika

to serve
3 ciabatta loaves
bulb of garlic
olive oil
4 large carrots
4 sticks celery

making the salsa verde dip
1 Put the parsley, sorrel, garlic, capers and chilli oil into a food processor. Whizz to a rough paste.
2 Add the cheese, soured cream, lemon juice and pepper to the processor and blend well.
3 Pour into a serving dish and chill; the dip may be runny after processing but will firm up after chilling.

making the yellow pepper dip
1 Grill the pieces of pepper, skin side up, until the skin is charred and blistered. Place the peppers in a plastic bag and fasten the top. Set aside for a few minutes.
2 Take the pepper out of the bag and peel off the skin. Roughly chop the flesh and place in a food processor with the garlic and chilli oil. Whizz to a coarse paste.
3 Add the cheese, soured cream, lemon juice and paprika to the processor and blend well. Pour into a serving dish and chill.

to serve
1 To make the bruschetta, cut the ciabatta into slices, about 2cm (¾in) thick, and toast, in batches, on both sides. While still hot, rub one side of each slice with a peeled clove of garlic. Then brush the other sides with olive oil.
2 Peel the carrots and trim the celery. Cut both into sticks for crudités.

smoked salmon terrine
with warm green salad

This luxurious terrine makes a magnificent centrepiece for any occasion. Cut it into slices to reveal the layers of luscious smoked salmon and dill-flavoured butter; or you could serve small portions on slices of bread or bruschetta.

Cook's notes

This recipe uses marinated anchovies as well as herbs and lemon juice and zest to flavour the butter. Don't use canned anchovies because you will find they are too salty for this particular dish. You should be able to purchase marinated anchovies at the delicatessen counter in most major supermarkets.

you will need

preparation time *30 minutes plus overnight chilling*

cooking time *5-10 minutes*

for the terrine

1-1.5kg (2lb 4oz-3lb 5oz) sliced smoked salmon

175g (6oz) unsalted butter

55g (2oz) marinated anchovies

finely grated zest of 1 lemon

juice of ½ lemon

2 tbsp chopped fresh dill

salt and pepper

for the warm green salad

300ml (10fl oz) olive oil

4 lemons, cut into wedges

salt and pepper

6-8 courgettes, cut in diagonal slices

450g (1lb) sugar snap peas

2 heads fennel

30g packet flatleaf parsley

225g bag baby spinach

2 bunches watercress

making the terrine

1 Line a 900g (2lb) loaf tin or 1.4 litre (2½ pint) terrine dish with plastic wrap.

2 Beat the butter until very soft. Cut the anchovies into about 3mm (⅛in) dice and beat into the butter with the lemon zest and juice. Mix in the dill and season. Set aside at room temperature.

3 Line the loaf tin or dish with salmon slices, making sure there is an overhang of about 5cm (2in) around the sides. Cover the bottom with more smoked salmon and then smear over a thin layer of the butter. Cover the butter with more salmon. Continue layering until the tin is full, finishing with a layer of salmon.

4 Fold the overhanging salmon over the layered salmon. Cover with plastic wrap. Place another loaf tin, weighed down with a couple of small tins, or another terrine dish, on top – this will help press the layers together. Refrigerate for several hours, preferably overnight.

5 To serve, remove from the fridge and turn out. Take off the plastic wrap and slice while still chilled.

preparing the salad

1 To make the dressing, heat 3 tbsp oil in a frying-pan over moderate heat and fry the lemon until the edges begin to colour. Take off the heat and stir in the remaining oil; season to taste and set aside.

2 Bring a large pan of salted water to the boil and drop in the courgettes and sugar snap peas. Cook for 1-2 minutes until the courgettes are slightly softened. Drain and refresh under cold-running water. Set aside, at room temperature, until needed.

3 Trim and shred the fennel. Pull the parsley leaves off the stalks and place in a bowl with the spinach, fennel, watercress and blanched vegetables.

4 Take the lemon out of the oil and then pour the dressing over the salad. Mix together well and serve at once with the lemon wedges.

1 Put the redcurrants, blackcurrants and raspberries into separate saucepans. Divide the sugar between the 3 saucepans.

2 Thoroughly mix the crème de cassis with 150ml (5fl oz) water. Pour 100ml (3½fl oz) of this liquid in with the redcurrants, another 100ml (3½fl oz) in with the blackcurrants and the remainder in with the raspberries. Stir each pan to mix the fruit with the sugar and liquid.

3 Put the pans over medium heat and bring them to the boil. Reduce the heat to low and cook the raspberries gently for 2-3 minutes until the fruit is just softened. Cook the redcurrants and blackcurrants for 5-7 minutes until the skins begin to burst. Set aside to cool.

4 Cut the brioche slices into small triangles and toast on each side. Set aside to cool.

5 Put 1 or 2 brioche triangles in the base of the serving glasses, which should be large and thick. Divide the raspberries between the glasses. Cover the layer of raspberries in each glass with a few more brioche triangles.

6 Divide the redcurrants between the glasses and top these with more brioche triangles. Finish with a layer of blackcurrants.

to serve

Divide the extra redcurrants into small bunches. Pour a little icing sugar into a bowl. Hold up a bunch of redcurrants by the stalk and brush the fruit lightly with the beaten egg white. Dip the redcurrants into the icing sugar and set aside. Repeat until they have all been dipped. Serve the summer puddings decorated with the frosted fruit.

lazy summer puddings

These stylish desserts have all the juiciness of a traditional summer pudding and are quick to make. Served in easy-to-hold wine glasses, they are just right for a leisurely buffet.

you will need

preparation time 25 minutes
plus chilling

cooking time 10 minutes

900g (2lb) redcurrants, trimmed, plus a few extra bunches to decorate
900g (2lb) blackcurrants, trimmed
900g (2lb) raspberries
500g (1lb 2oz) caster sugar
100ml (3½fl oz) crème de cassis
2 brioche loaves, cut into slices about 1cm (½in) thick
2-3 egg whites, lightly beaten
icing sugar

Thanksgiving dinner

serves 8

corn chowder

roast turkey
with sweet potatoes and
pecan cranberry stuffing

pecan pie

Thanksgiving dinner is the most popular of celebrations in America, commemorating the first harvest gathered by the new settlers. Corn chowder provides a wholesome prelude to the classic roast turkey with pecan cranberry stuffing. The meal ends on a high note with pecan pie – this one is as good as any you'd eat in the US of A!

Shopping list

225g (8oz) potatoes
900g (2lb) sweet potatoes
675g (1½lb) green beans
2 celery stalks
1 small green pepper; 1 small red pepper
fresh chives
225g (8oz) fresh cranberries
1 small orange
1 lemon
450g (1lb) frozen sweetcorn kernels
3.6kg (8lb) oven-ready turkey
6-8 rashers of bacon
425ml (15fl oz) chicken stock (see page 10)
300ml (10fl oz) single cream
225g (8oz) butter
55g (2oz) grated suet or butter
5 eggs
3 tbsp milk
190g (6½oz) caster sugar
115g (4oz) soft brown sugar
125g (4½oz) breadcrumbs
2 tbsp flour
2 tsp paprika
115g (4oz) dried cranberries
280g (10oz) pecan nuts
225g (8oz) sweet shortcrust pastry (see page 8, 'variations')
300ml (10fl oz) golden syrup
freshly grated nutmeg
1 tsp cinnamon
few drops of vanilla essence
6-8 tbsp medium sherry or rum
crème fraîche or clotted cream, to serve

Prepare ahead

The day before

Defrost the turkey
Make the chowder and chill in the fridge
Bake the pastry shell for the pecan pie

On the day

4 hours before guests arrive

Make the stuffing and leave it to cool
Pre-heat the oven for the pie
Make the pecan pie filling and bake the pie

2½-3hours before guests arrive

Put the turkey in the oven

1 hour before guests arrive

Put the sweet potatoes in the oven to roast

Just before serving the starter

Put the chowder on to reheat
Put a pan of water on to boil for cooking the beans

Between the starter and main course

Make the gravy from the pan juices (see page 10)
Cook the green beans
Put the pecan pie in a low oven to warm gently

corn chowder

This heartwarming soup is excellent for cold winter nights – and just right for getting a Thanksgiving evening off to a good start.

you will need
preparation time
15 minutes

cooking time *30 minutes*

450g (1lb) frozen sweetcorn kernels

225g (8oz) potatoes, finely diced

2 celery stalks, very finely chopped

1 small green pepper, very finely chopped

1 small red pepper, very finely chopped

55g (2oz) butter

1½ tsp salt

2 tbsp flour

2 tsp paprika

425ml (15fl oz) chicken stock (see page 10)

300ml (10fl oz) single cream

fresh chives

1 Heat the butter in a large saucepan and add the potatoes, celery, peppers and salt. Fry for about 10 minutes until softened, stirring frequently to prevent them from sticking.
2 Stir in the flour and paprika and keep stirring until they are blended. Cook for 1 minute.

3 Pour in the chicken stock and cook over a medium heat, stirring continuously, for about 5 minutes until the mixture is smooth and thick.
4 Stir in the corn kernels and half the cream and cook on a low to medium heat, stirring frequently, for 10 minutes.
5 Serve the soup in bowls, garnished with cream and a sprinkling of chives.

roast turkey
with sweet potatoes and pecan cranberry stuffing

Traditional Thanksgiving turkey makes a tasty meal at any time. Serve it with roasted sweet potatoes, green beans and gravy made from the pan juices (see page 10). For an extra flavour, try the bright cranberry relish.

you will need

preparation time *50 minutes*
cooking time *3-3½ hours*

3.6kg (8lb) oven-ready turkey
large knob of butter, softened
6-8 rashers of bacon
salt and pepper

for the stuffing

125g (4½oz) breadcrumbs
55g (2oz) grated suet or butter
115g (4oz) dried cranberries soaked in orange juice or water
grated zest of 1 lemon
55g (2oz) pecan nuts, chopped
1 egg yolk
3 tbsp milk
salt and pepper

for the sweet potatoes

900g (2lb) sweet potatoes, peeled and sliced into 1cm (½in) slices
115g (4oz) butter
115g (4oz) soft brown sugar
1 tsp cinnamon
freshly grated nutmeg
6-8 tbsp medium sherry or rum

for the green beans

675g (1½lb) green beans, topped and tailed
knob of butter

stuffing the turkey

1 Make sure the turkey is defrosted and the cavity is clean.
2 Mix all the stuffing ingredients thoroughly in a large bowl.
3 Stuff the neck of the turkey with one third of the stuffing.

roasting the turkey

1 Pre-heat the oven to 220°C/425°F/gas 7.
2 Rub butter over the breast of the turkey and season. Lay the bacon over the upper breast of the bird.
3 Spread the remaining stuffing in a buttered baking dish and refrigerate.
4 Put the turkey in the oven and cook for 30 minutes. Reduce the temperature to 180°C/350°F/gas 4 and roast for a further 2½-3 hours, basting regularly. About 50 minutes before the end of cooking, put the stuffing in the oven.
5 To check the turkey is done, pierce one thigh with a skewer – the juices

Recipe option

cranberry orange relish

1 small orange, peeled
225g (8oz) fresh cranberries
115g (4oz) caster sugar

1 Cut the orange into chunks and blitz quickly.
2 Add the cranberries and process again until the mixture is pulped but still chunky.
3 Add the sugar and pulse until blended. Serve in a small bowl.

should run clear. Transfer the bird from the roasting tin to a serving dish and leave in a warm place to rest.

roasting the sweet potatoes

1 Heat half the butter in a frying-pan and sauté the sweet potato slices on both sides until they turn golden brown.
2 Generously butter a large baking dish or roasting tin. Arrange the potato slices in a single layer in the tin, sprinkle with the sugar, dot with the remaining butter and sprinkle with cinnamon and nutmeg.
3 Pour the sherry or rum over the top and put the potatoes in the oven with the turkey.
4 Cook for 40 minutes or until tender, turning the slices halfway through cooking.

cooking the green beans

Put the beans in a large pan of lightly salted boiling water. Cook for 2-3 minutes, drain and toss in butter.

pecan pie

This most American of puddings is the perfect Thanksgiving dessert – the crisp pastry with its toffee-nut filling is sublime, especially when served with crème fraîche or clotted cream.

you will need

preparation time *35 minutes*

cooking time *45 minutes*

225g (8oz) sweet shortcrust pastry (see page 8, 'variations')

225g (8oz) pecan nuts

4 eggs

175g (6oz) caster sugar

300ml (10fl oz) golden syrup

pinch of salt

few drops of vanilla essence

crème fraîche or clotted cream, to serve

1 Pre-heat the oven to 190°C/375°F/gas 5 and grease a 20cm (8in) flan tin.

2 Roll out the sweet pastry quite thinly and use it to line the flan tin. Line the pastry with greaseproof paper, fill with baking beans and bake in the pre-heated oven for 15-20 minutes.

3 Remove the beans and the paper and leave the pastry case to cool.

4 Increase the oven temperature to 200°C/400°F/gas 6.

5 Beat the eggs lightly in a bowl, then whisk in the sugar, syrup, salt and vanilla essence. Stir in the pecan nuts.

6 Pour the mixture into the partly cooked flan case and bake in the oven for 10 minutes.

7 Reduce the oven temperature to 180°C/350°F/gas 4 and bake the pie for a further 35 minutes until set. If the pastry starts to singe towards the end of cooking, cover the top of the tart with a sheet of foil.

8 Allow the pie to cool and firm up a little before serving it warm, with a generous helping of crème fraîche or clotted cream.

feast of flavours

serves 8

peppered chicken livers
on watercress toasts

spinach and cheddar mushrooms
smoked trout and potato salad
chorizo and chick-peas

apricot-lime sponge pie

This menu mirrors the concept of Spanish tapas – it gives everyone the opportunity to dip into several different dishes and experience a wide variety of flavours. The spread offers something for everyone – vegetarians and meat-eaters alike – plus a lovely fruit pudding to round it off.

Shopping list

450g (1lb) fresh spinach
450g (1lb) small new potatoes
12 medium-sized open-cup mushrooms
6 large tomatoes
2 medium onions; 2 small onions; 1 red onion
2 shallots; 2 cloves of garlic
1 large bunch of watercress
large bag of mixed salad leaves
salad vegetables of your choice
bunches of parsley and coriander
1 lime; 1 lemon
400g (14oz) fresh apricots
350g (12oz) smoked trout fillets
450g (1lb) chicken livers
175g (6oz) chorizo
115g (4oz) grated cheddar cheese
225g (8oz) unsalted butter
double cream or ice-cream
icing sugar
2 eggs
milk
2 x 400g (14oz) cans chick-peas
175-225g (6-8oz) sweet shortcrust pastry
(see page 8, 'variations')
2-4 tbsp lime marmalade
loaf of white bread
55g (2oz) caster sugar; demerara sugar
55g (2oz) plain or self-raising flour
4 tsp Dijon mustard; 9 tbsp tomato ketchup
3 tbsp Worcestershire sauce; Tabasco sauce
4 tbsp mayonnaise (see page 187)
English mustard powder; horseradish sauce
white wine vinegar
150ml (5fl oz) extra virgin olive oil
olive oil; vegetable oil
55ml (2fl oz) brandy

Prepare ahead

The day before

Soak the chicken livers in milk
Make the spicy tomato dressing
Make the mustard mayonnaise

On the day

4 hours before guests arrive

Boil the potatoes for the smoked trout salad and leave them to cool
Stamp out the bread circles (keep in plastic wrap in the fridge) and use the remainder of the slices for making fine fresh breadcrumbs for the peppered chicken livers

2-3 hours before guests arrive

Prepare the simple salad and the smoked trout and potato salad
Make the topping for the mushrooms, then grill and fill the mushrooms
Mix the mustard dressing for the peppered chicken livers
Make the apricot-lime sponge pie

1 hour before guests arrive

Make the chorizo and chick-peas, cover and keep warm in the oven

30 minutes before guests arrive

Dress the watercress for the peppered chicken livers with olive oil and seasoning
Toss the mixed salad leaves and vegetables in the spicy tomato dressing

Just before sitting down to eat

Sprinkle grated cheese on top of the filled mushrooms and brown under the grill
Fry the chicken livers and toast the bread; assemble the peppered chicken livers

Recipe option
mustard dressing

knob of butter
½ tsp demerara sugar
2 tbsp finely chopped shallots
55ml (2fl oz) brandy
1 egg yolk
4 tsp Dijon mustard
2 tbsp white wine vinegar
8 tbsp olive oil
4 tbsp vegetable oil
salt and pepper

1 Melt the butter and sugar in a pan and fry the chopped shallots for 2-3 minutes.
2 Add the brandy and reduce for 2-3 minutes until almost dry, then cool.
3 Mix the mustard, egg yolk and vinegar in a bowl and slowly whisk in the two oils. Season.

peppered chicken livers
on watercress toasts

The crisp garlicky toast goes wonderfully well with the rich chicken livers and peppery, crunchy watercress. The mustard dressing makes these bite-sized wonders even tastier.

you will need
preparation time
30 minutes
soaking time *24-48 hours*
cooking time *10 minutes*

450g (1lb) chicken livers, soaked for 24-48 hours in milk
6-8 slices of bread
1 garlic clove, halved

salt and 2 tsp coarsely ground black pepper
1 large bunch watercress
2 tbsp olive oil
knob of butter

1 Remove the chicken livers from the milk.
2 Cut 4 discs out of each slice of bread with a plain biscuit cutter. Rub each disc with garlic and toast under a hot grill.
3 Make fine breadcrumbs from the leftover bread. Measure out 6-8 tbsp of the breadcrumbs and combine them with a little salt and the pepper.
4 Dress the watercress with half the olive oil and a little salt and pepper.

5 Heat the remaining oil and butter in a frying-pan.
6 Roll the livers in the peppered crumbs and pan-fry them until crisp and golden – about 3-5 minutes depending on the size.
7 Sit the toasted discs on a large plate and top each with the watercress and chicken liver.

a profusion of dishes
with salad leaves and vegetables in a spicy dressing

Present your guests with an array of flavours – mushrooms topped with cheese, smoked trout and potato salad pepped up with mustard mayo plus savoury chorizo and chick-peas. Serve with salad leaves and vegetables in a spicy tomato dressing.

spinach and cheddar mushrooms
you will need

450g (1lb) fresh spinach, washed and stalks removed
115g (4oz) grated cheddar cheese
12 medium-sized open-cup mushrooms, stalks removed and saved
olive or vegetable oil
15g (½oz) butter
2 small onions, thinly sliced
salt and pepper

1 Cook the damp spinach in a large pan for about 2 minutes until it has wilted. Drain well and chop coarsely.
2 Pre-heat the grill to medium. Lay the mushrooms, gill side up, on a lightly greased baking sheet. Season and trickle over a little oil. Grill for 4-5 minutes until tender.
3 Melt the butter in a frying-pan. Slice the mushroom stalks and fry with the onions until golden.
4 Stir in the spinach and season.
5 Spoon the mix on top of the mushrooms and sprinkle with cheese. Grill until bubbling.

smoked trout and potato salad
you will need

350g (12oz) smoked trout fillets, flaked
450g (1lb) small new potatoes
1 red onion, finely chopped
1 tbsp olive oil
squeeze of lemon juice
1 tsp chopped fresh parsley
salt and pepper

for the mustard mayonnaise
4 tbsp mayonnaise (see page 187)
½ tsp English mustard powder
1 tsp horseradish sauce
pinch of salt

1 Combine all the ingredients for the mayonnaise in a bowl and set aside.
2 Boil the potatoes for 10-12 minutes or until tender, leave them to cool, then cut in half.
3 Mix the potatoes with the red onion, olive oil, lemon juice, parsley, mustard mayonnaise and seasoning. Stir in the flakes of smoked trout.
4 Put on a serving dish and drizzle with a little more olive oil.

chorizo and chick-peas
you will need

1 tbsp olive oil
2 onions, finely chopped
1 garlic clove, crushed
175g (6oz) chorizo, cut into thin slices
2 x 400g (14oz) canned chick-peas
6 large tomatoes, chopped
2 tbsp chopped parsley
2 tbsp chopped coriander
salt and pepper

1 Heat the oil in a pan, add the onion and fry for 5-7 minutes until soft.
2 Add the garlic and chorizo. Cook until the sausage browns (pour off some oil if there is too much).
3 Drain and rinse the chick-peas and add to the onion and sausage.
4 Add the tomatoes, parsley and coriander and cook over a medium heat for 5-6 minutes. Season.

spicy tomato dressing
you will need

9 tbsp tomato ketchup
125ml (4fl oz) white wine vinegar
3 tbsp Worcestershire sauce
a few drops of Tabasco sauce
150ml (5fl oz) extra virgin olive oil
150ml (5fl oz) olive oil
freshly milled salt and pepper
mixed salad leaves and vegetables of your choice

1 Mix together the ketchup, vinegar, Worcestershire and Tabasco sauces.
2 Gradually whisk in the oils and season to taste.
3 Toss a selection of salad leaves and vegetables in the dressing.

apricot-lime sponge pie

This is a very flexible recipe – if you can't find apricots, use plums, cherries, damsons or greengages instead. It's lovely served warm or cold with double cream or ice-cream.

you will need

preparation time *30 minutes*

cooking time *1 hour*

175-225g (6-8oz) sweet shortcrust pastry (see page 8, 'variations'), rolled out thinly

400g (14oz) fresh apricots, halved and stoned

2-3 tbsp lime marmalade

55g (2oz) unsalted butter

55g (2oz) caster sugar

1 egg

55g (2oz) plain flour (or use self-raising for a lighter finish)

grated zest and juice of 1 lime

double cream or ice-cream, to serve

for the glaze (optional)

1 tbsp lime marmalade or apricot jam

icing sugar, for dusting

1 Pre-heat the oven to 200°C/400°F/gas 6. Grease a 20cm (8in) loose-bottomed flan tin.

2 Line the flan tin with the pastry, leaving a little hanging over the edge.

3 Line the pastry with greaseproof paper and baking beans. Bake for 20 minutes. Remove from the oven and remove the beans and paper. Trim off excess pastry around the rim.

4 If the apricots are ripe, they are ready to use, but if they're firm put them on a baking tray, skin side down, and dust generously with icing sugar. To soften them, cook in the pre-heated oven for 4-6 minutes.

5 Reduce the oven temperature to 180°C/350°F/gas 4.

6 Make the sponge by creaming together the butter and sugar. Beat in the egg slowly and fold in the flour with the zest of the lime. Then add the lime juice.

7 Spread the marmalade over the base of the pastry shell. Then spoon the sponge mix on top and level it out. Sit the apricots, skin side up, on top of the sponge. Bake in the oven for 35-40 minutes. When cooked, remove from the oven and leave for 10 minutes before serving.

glazing the pie

If you want to glaze the pie, heat the marmalade or jam with 2 tbsp water and brush over the top of the fruit. Finish off with a good dusting of icing sugar.

party
light bites

serves 15-20

parmesan risotto bites

pepper and anchovy toasts

crispy potato skins
with sour cream salsa dip

spicy turkey pastries

Finger food is perfect for big celebrations. To make a change from traditional party snacks, here's a lively selection of delectable savoury bites, which taste fabulous served either warm or cold. For a real party atmosphere, offer your guests a choice of cocktails – buck's fizz or kir.

Shopping list

5-6 large baking potatoes
2 large onions; 2 red onions
1 shallot
2 red peppers
2 green chillies
2 garlic cloves
1 lemon and 1 lime
8 ripe tomatoes
fresh coriander, tarragon, parsley and basil
85g (3oz) unsalted butter
142ml carton soured cream
4 tbsp grated parmesan
6 eggs
500g (1lb 20z) puff pastry (see page 9)
12 marinated anchovy fillets
450g (1lb) cold cooked turkey
1.2 litres (2 pints) chicken stock (see page 10)
225g (8oz) arborio or carnaroli rice
5-6 tbsp plain flour
5-6 tbsp fine white breadcrumbs
10 slices white bread
white pepper and black peppercorns
sun-dried tomatoes
2-3 tbsp curry paste
coriander seeds
white wine vinegar
vegetable oil for frying
150ml (5fl oz) extra virgin olive oil
330ml (11fl oz) olive oil
sea salt; rock salt

Prepare ahead

A week before

Make the vierge dressing and store in a screw-top jar, shaking contents daily

On the day

4 hours before guests arrive

Bake the potatoes, leave to go cold, then cut into wedges and scoop out the flesh
Make the mayonnaise and pastry for the spicy turkey pastries

3 hours before guests arrive

Make the risotto and leave to cool

2 hours before guests arrive

Skin the peppers and leave to marinate in the vierge dressing
Mix up the curried turkey mayonnaise

1 hour before guests arrive

Make the salsa sour cream dip
Form the risotto into balls and refrigerate
Bake the pastry squares

30-15 minutes before guests arrive

Stir the anchovies into the pepper mix; toast the bread
Deep-fry the potato skins and sprinkle with salt
Deep-fry the risotto balls
Spoon the curried turkey mayonnaise on to the pastry squares

parmesan risotto bites

Rich, slightly glutinous risotto is bound with parmesan and perked up with fresh parsley and sun-dried tomatoes. Formed into balls and deep-fried, this makes appetizing party fare.

you will need

preparation time
45 minutes plus 1 hour chilling

makes 35-40 risotto bites
85g (3oz) unsalted butter
1 tbsp olive oil
2 large onions, finely chopped
1.2 litres (2 pints) chicken stock (see page 10)
225g (8oz) arborio or carnaroli rice
4 tbsp finely grated parmesan
1 tbsp finely chopped fresh parsley
2 tbsp finely chopped sun-dried tomatoes
salt and pepper
vegetable oil for frying
5-6 tbsp plain flour
2 eggs, beaten
5-6 tbsp fine white breadcrumbs

1 Melt the butter with the olive oil in a large pan. Add the chopped onions and cook gently for a few minutes, without colouring, until soft.
2 Meanwhile, bring the stock to a simmer.

3 Add the rice to the onions and continue to cook for a few minutes, stirring occasionally.
4 Add the hot stock to the rice a ladleful at a time, allowing the risotto to simmer gently. When the stock has been absorbed by the rice, add another ladleful. Continue this process, stirring almost continuously to maintain even cooking and prevent the rice from sticking. The risotto will take 20-25 minutes to cook. Make sure there is still a slight bite left in the rice at the end.
5 Stir in the parmesan, parsley and tomatoes. Season with salt and pepper. Allow to cool.
6 Shape the risotto into balls about 4cm (1½in) in diameter and sit on a floured tray. Refrigerate for an hour to firm up.
7 Heat the oil in a deep-fat fryer or deep frying-pan to 180°C/350°F/gas 4. Roll the balls in the flour, egg and breadcrumbs and deep-fry for 3-4 minutes until golden and crispy. Drain on kitchen paper. Serve warm or cold, garnished with parsley.

tasty mini dishes

pepper and anchovy toasts and crispy potato skins

Marinated, oiled anchovies are best suited to this recipe, not the canned variety (see 'Cook's notes' page 194). If you can't buy the right kind, use peppers only. The golden crispy potato skins go beautifully with a dip made from spicy salsa mixed with soured cream.

pepper and anchovy toasts
you will need
preparation time *30 minutes*
marinating time *several days for the dressing; 1-2 hours for the peppers*

makes about 20 toasts
2 red peppers, halved and deseeded
12 marinated anchovy fillets
10 slices white bread
basil sprigs, to garnish

for the vierge dressing
150ml (5fl oz) extra virgin olive oil
1 tsp coriander seeds, crushed
1 tbsp fresh tarragon
3 black peppercorns, crushed
1 shallot, finely chopped
1 garlic clove, crushed
pinch of sea salt

making the vierge dressing
1 Warm the extra virgin olive oil with the coriander seeds in a small pan. Place the remaining dressing ingredients in a screw-top jar and pour the warm oil and coriander over them.
2 Screw on the lid and leave to marinate for a week, shaking the bottle daily.

making the pepper mixture
1 Pre-heat the grill to hot. Lay the red pepper halves, skin side up, on the grill rack. Grill them until the skins are blackened all over.
2 Seal the charred peppers in a plastic bag for 15 minutes. When cool enough to handle, peel them and cut into thin strips.
3 Douse the pepper strips with 2-3 tbsp of the vierge dressing, cover and leave for 1-2 hours to marinate.
4 Just before serving, split the anchovy fillets in half lengthways and slice widthways. Mix with the peppers.

to serve
Toast the bread and cut into small pieces. Top each piece with a spoonful of the pepper and anchovy mix and garnish with a sprig of basil.

deep-fried crispy potato skins with sour cream salsa dip
you will need
preparation time *15-20 minutes*

makes 30-48 wedges
5-6 large baked potatoes
vegetable oil for frying
rock salt

for the dip
8 ripe tomatoes, deseeded and finely diced
2 red onions, finely diced
1 garlic clove, finely chopped
2 green chillies, deseeded and finely chopped
1 x 142ml carton soured cream
1 lime
salt and pepper

frying the potato skins
1 Cut each baked potato into 6-8 wedges. Scoop out the potato flesh, leaving 2-3mm (⅛in) of potato attached to the skin.
2 Heat the oil to 180°C/350°F/gas 4 in a deep-fat fryer or deep frying-pan. Deep-fry the skins in batches until golden and crispy. Drain and sprinkle with rock salt.

making the dip
Mix the tomatoes, onion, garlic and chilli into the soured cream. Add a few squeezes of lime juice and plenty of salt and pepper.

to serve
Arrange the salted potato wedges on a large plate with a bowl of the salsa dip in the middle.

Recipe option

buck's fizz

300ml (10fl oz) fresh orange juice
champagne
handful of ice

Put the ice in a large jug and add the orange juice. Fill up the jug with champagne.

kir

dry white wine
crème de cassis
ice (optional)

Put 1 tsp crème de cassis into a wine glass and top up with dry white wine. Some people like it with ice.

spicy turkey pastries

These bite-sized savouries turn roast turkey into something deliciously different. For variety, serve some with and some without their pastry lids.

you will need
preparation time *30 minutes*
cooking time *10 minutes*

makes about 30 pastries
500g (1lb 20z) puff pastry (see page 9)
1 egg, beaten
450g (1lb) cold roast turkey, diced
fresh chopped coriander, to serve

for the mayonnaise
3 egg yolks
1 tbsp white wine vinegar
salt and white pepper
300ml (10fl oz) olive oil
squeeze of lemon juice
2-3 tbsp curry paste

making the mayonnaise
1 Whisk the egg yolks, vinegar and seasoning together in a liquidizer or food processor; then slowly add the olive oil while whisking continuously.
2 Whisk in 1 tsp hot water, add the lemon juice and check the seasoning. Cover and chill in the fridge.

baking the pastry
1 Pre-heat the oven to 200°C/400°F/gas 6. Butter a baking sheet.
2 Roll out the pastry thinly. Trim the edges and cut into 6cm (2½in) squares. With a knife, mark a smaller square – about 4cm (1½in) – in each pastry square (don't cut right through).
3 Place the squares on the baking tray, glaze with the beaten egg and bake for about 10 minutes until risen and golden (you may need to do this in batches). Cool on a wire rack then remove the top of the inner squares, leaving hollows for the filling.

assembling the pastries
1 Just before serving, mix together the mayonnaise and curry paste; then stir in the turkey.
2 Spoon the mixture into the pastry squares and sprinkle with coriander.

celebration dinner

serves 6-8

tomato-mozzarella salad

cullen skink
smoked haddock and potato soup

berry crumble
with whipped cream

This simple menu of subtle flavours makes an great celebration dinner, whatever the occasion. Start the party in style with champagne cocktails to get your guests in the mood for a refreshing tomato-mozzarella salad, and a creamy fish soup. The crumble dessert is fabulous.

Shopping list

6 beefsteak tomatoes
12-18 cherry tomatoes
2 shallots
1 garlic clove
1 large onion
675g (1½lb) floury potatoes
350g (12oz) leeks
450g (1lb) fresh or frozen blueberries
450g (1lb) fresh or frozen blackberries
1 lemon
1 packet fresh basil leaves or fresh chives
small bunch fresh parsley
1.3kg (3lb) undyed smoked haddock fillets
225g (8oz) mozzarella cheese
600ml (1 pint) milk
225ml (8fl oz) single cream
140g (5oz) butter
5 large eggs
4-5 tbsp soft, light brown sugar
115g (4oz) demerara sugar
caster sugar; sugar lumps
175g (6oz) wholemeal flour
85g (3oz) pecan or walnut halves
16 black olives
whole nutmeg
ground cinnamon
double cream or custard
1-2 loaves crusty bread or cheese scones (see page 218)
8 tbsp olive oil
3 tbsp balsamic vinegar
brandy
Angostura bitters (optional)
champagne

Prepare ahead

On the day

In the morning

Make the crumble topping and cover until needed

Cook the fruit for the blueberry and blackberry crumble, if required (see 'Cook's notes' on page 220) and leave to cool

Poach the haddock and make the soup up to the end of step 4. Put the flaked haddock flesh in a covered dish and keep in a cold place until needed

Make the salad dressing

Put the champagne in the fridge to chill

1 hour before guests arrive

Make the salad and drizzle with a little of the dressing

If using uncooked berries for the crumble, mix them with the sugar and lemon juice

Just before guests arrive

Put the salad and the dressing on the table to adjust to room temperature

Top the fruits with the crumble mix and put into the oven to bake

Put the sugar lumps and brandy in the champagne glasses

Just before sitting down to eat

Check the crumble is cooked (golden brown on top); turn off the oven. Leave the crumble in the oven to keep warm

Between the starter and main course

Reheat the soup and finish off with the cream, egg yolk, flaked fish and parsley

Cut thick slices of bread to serve with the soup

Between the main course and pudding

Whip the cream to go with the crumble

(See page 214 for some more cocktails.)

Recipe option
champagne cocktail

champagne
sugar lumps
brandy
Angostura bitters (optional)

Put 1 sugar lump and 1 tsp brandy into each glass. Fill up with champagne. If you like, add a few drops of Angostura bitters too.

arranging the salad
1 Cut the stalk end out of each beefsteak tomato with a sharp, pointed knife. Then slice the beefsteak tomatoes and arrange in overlapping circles on a large flat plate (leaving space in the centre for the eggs). Sprinkle with a tiny amount of sugar.
2 Slice the mozzarella cheese and tuck a disc between each slice of beefsteak tomato.
3 Cut the cherry tomatoes into halves and arrange them on top of the cheese and tomato slices.
4 Scatter the olives and shallots over the tomatoes.
5 Quarter the eggs and arrange in the centre of the plate. Sprinkle basil leaves or snipped chives over the whole salad.
6 Drizzle a little of the dressing over the salad about 30 minutes before serving. Serve the rest in a jug with the salad.

tomato-mozzarella salad

This colourful salad is made with two types of tomato, beefsteak and cherry. If you can find it, creamy mozzarella made from buffalo's milk makes a difference to the salad's texture.

you will need
preparation time
20 minutes

for the dressing
8 tbsp olive oil
3 tbsp balsamic vinegar
1 garlic clove, crushed
salt and pepper

for the salad
6 beefsteak tomatoes
caster sugar, for sprinkling
225g (8oz) mozzarella cheese
12-18 cherry tomatoes
2 shallots, peeled and very finely chopped
16 black olives, stoned

4 large eggs, hard-boiled
basil leaves or snipped chives to garnish

making the dressing
Put all the dressing ingredients into a screw-top jar and shake until well blended.

cullen skink
smoked haddock and potato soup

This wonderfully savoury fish soup is robust enough for a main course. The flavours are fresh but creamy and you can finish the soup with a little butter for extra richness. Serve it with cheese scones or fresh, crusty bread.

Cook's notes

Cullen skink is a soup that is a speciality from the Moray Firth on the east coast of Scotland. 'Skink' signifies a hearty stew-like soup, which is exactly what this is. For authenticity, try to find genuine Finnan haddock, which gives a distinctive flavour. Don't use bright yellow dyed haddock – the natural undyed variety is far superior.

you will need

preparation time 15 minutes
cooking time 30-35 minutes

1.3kg (3lb) undyed smoked haddock fillets
1 large onion, peeled and diced
600ml (1 pint) milk
675g (1½lb) floury potatoes, peeled and diced
350g (12oz) leeks, trimmed, washed and chopped
225ml (8fl oz) single cream
1 egg yolk
pepper (and salt if needed)
2 tbsp chopped fresh parsley
55g (2oz) butter (optional)
1-2 loaves crusty bread or cheese scones (see 'Recipe option'), to serve

1 Put the haddock in a shallow pan with the onion, milk and 600ml (1 pint) water and bring just to the boil. Reduce the heat, cover the pan and poach the fish gently, without boiling, for 7-10 minutes.
2 Lift the haddock carefully from the liquid, drain, then remove and discard the skin and bones. Flake the flesh and reserve. Pour the cooking liquor, with the onion, into a large saucepan or flameproof casserole dish.
3 Add the diced potatoes to the fish liquid, with the leeks, and bring to the boil.
4 Reduce the heat, cover and simmer for 10-15 minutes until the potatoes and leeks are tender. Mash a few of the potato pieces into the liquid with a fork to thicken the soup.
5 Whisk the cream and egg yolk together and stir into the soup. Reheat gently, stirring, until it thickens slightly, but do not boil or the soup will curdle.
6 Stir in the flaked haddock and season to taste with pepper, and salt if needed (the smoked haddock will probably provide enough salt). Stir in the chopped parsley and heat through for 2-3 minutes.
7 Serve the soup in a large heated tureen or in the flameproof casserole. If you like, dot with knobs of butter which will melt over the surface of the soup.

Recipe option
cheese scones

225kg (8oz) self-raising flour
1 tsp baking powder
½ tsp mustard powder
pinch of salt
25g (1oz) butter
55g (2oz) grated cheddar cheese plus extra to serve
1 egg, beaten
4-5 tbsp milk

1 Pre-heat the oven to 220°C/425°F/gas 7.
2 Sift together the flour, baking powder, mustard powder and salt. Add the butter and rub in.
3 Add the cheese, egg and milk and mix to a smooth dough, adding more milk if necessary.
4 Roll out the dough to 2cm (¾in) thick; cut into rounds with a cookie cutter. Put on a buttered baking sheet, sprinkle with cheese and bake for 15 minutes.

Cook's notes

If you like your fruit very soft, you can cook the filling in advance. Bring the berries, sugar and lemon juice to a simmer and cook for 3-4 minutes. Pour into the pie dish and leave to cool completely. Make the topping – this can also be done beforehand – and spoon it on to the berries. Bake for about 20 minutes – the fruit is already cooked so it requires a little less baking.

Tip

If you can't buy fresh berries from the supermarket, frozen ones are a good substitute. Make sure you defrost them completely before use. You can also use tinned fruit, but drain at least half the liquid away or the filling will be too wet.

berry crumble

Dark and delicious, blueberries and blackberries combine beautifully with a crunchy, nutty, spicy crumble. Serve with whipped cream or custard.

you will need

preparation time *15 minutes*

cooking time *30 minutes*

450g (1lb) blueberries

450g (1lb) blackberries

4-5 tbsp soft, light brown sugar

1 tbsp lemon juice

85g (3oz) pecan or walnut halves, chopped

175g (6oz) wholemeal flour

85g (3oz) butter

115g (4oz) demerara sugar

zest of 1 lemon

freshly grated nutmeg

pinch of ground cinnamon

whipped double cream or custard, to serve

1 Pile the berries into a 1.4 litre (2½ pint) baking dish. Sprinkle evenly with light brown sugar and lemon juice.

2 Spread the nuts in a grill pan and toast under a hot grill for 3 minutes until just starting to brown – don't let them burn.

3 Sift the flour into a bowl and rub in the butter until the mix resembles breadcrumbs. Stir in the demerara sugar, toasted nuts and lemon zest. Flavour with a little freshly grated nutmeg and a pinch of cinnamon.

4 Spoon the crumble mix on top of the berries and press down lightly. Bake in a pre-heated oven at 190°C/375°F/gas 5 for 30 minutes until the top is golden brown. Serve warm with whipped double cream or custard.

index of recipes

index

acknowledgements

Photographs:
Back Cover: (top) Iain Bagwell, (centre) Thomas Odulate, (bottom) Ken Field.

Eaglemoss Publications (Karl Adamson) 8, 9, (Chris Alack) 11(bl), 25(tl,bl,br), 26(tr), 27(t), 28(tc), 29, 30(tl), 37(tl,bl,br), 38(tr), 39(t), 40(tc), 41, 42(tl), 79(t, bl), 93(tl,bl,br), 94(tr), 95(tl), 96(t), 97, 98(tl), 123(tl,bl,br), 124(tr), 125(tl), 126(t), 127, 128(tl), 203(tl,bl,br), 204(tr), 205, 206(t), 207, 208(tl), 209(tl,bl,br), 210(tr), 211(tl), 212(t), 213, 214(tl,tr), (Iain Bagwell) 2, 4(r), 11(br), 67(tl,bl,br), 68(tr), 69(t), 70(t), 71, 72(tl), 117(tl,bl,br), 118(tr), 119(tl), 120(t), 121, 122(t), 129(tl,bl,br), 130(tr), 131(tl), 132(tl), 133, 134(tl), 153(tl), 167, 179, 215(tl,bl,br), 216(tr), 217(tl), 218(tl), 219, 220(tl), (Steve Baxter) 10, 111(tl,bl,br), 112(t), 113(t), 114(t), 115, 116(t), (Martin Brigdale) 61(tl,bl,br), 62(tr), 63, 64(tr), 65, 66, (Ken Field) 43(tl,bl,br), 44(tr), 45(t), 46(t), 47, 48(t), 105(tl,br,bl), 106(tr), 107(tl), 108(t), 109, 110(tl), 141(tl,bl,br), 142(tr), 143(tl), 144(tc), 145, 146(tl), 153(bl), 185(tl,bl,br), 186(t), 187(t), 188(t), 189, 190, 197, (Gus Filgate) 4(l), 153(br), 155(tl,bl,br), 156(t), 157, 158(t), 159, 160(t), (Graham Kirk) 147, (William Lingwood) 87(tl,bl,br), 88(t), 89(t), 90(t), 91, 92, (Thomas Odulate) 11(t), 31(tl,bl,br), 32(tr), 33(tl), 34(t), 35, 36(tl), 73(tl,bl,br), 74(tr), 75(tl), 76(t), 77, 78(tl), 79(br), 81(tl,bl,br), 82(tr), 83(t), 84(t), 85, 86(tl), 135, 161(tl,bl,br), 162(t), 163(t), 164(t), 165(c), 166(t), 173(tl,bl,br), 174(tr), 175(tr), 176(tc,bl), 177(c), 178(tl), (William Reavell) 99(tl,bl,br), 100(tr), 101(t), 102(t), 103, 104(tl), (Howard Shooter) 55(bl), 58(t), 59, (Simon Smith) 4(c), 13(tl,bl,br), 14(tr), 15(tr), 16(t), 17(sp), 18(tl), 19(tl,bl,br), 20(tr), 21(tl), 22(t), 23, 24(tl), 49(tl,bl,br), 50(tr), 51(tl), 52(t), 53, 54(tl), 117(tl,bl,br,tr), 119(tl), 120(t), 121, 122(tl), 191, (Jon Whitaker) 55(tl,br), 56(t), 57(t), 60.